Table of Contents

I. Foreword

This year the Office of the United States Trade Representative (USTR) publishes its second annual *Report on Technical Barriers to Trade (TBT Report)*. This report was created to respond to the concerns of U.S. companies, farmers, ranchers and manufacturers, which increasingly encounter non-tariff trade barriers in the form of product standards, testing requirements, and other technical requirements as they seek to sell products and services around the world. As tariff barriers to industrial and agricultural trade have fallen, standards-related measures of this kind have emerged as a primary concern.

Governments, market participants and other entities can use standards-related measures as an effective and efficient means of achieving legitimate commercial and policy objectives. But when standards-related measures are outdated, overly burdensome, discriminatory, or otherwise inappropriate, these measures can reduce competition, stifle innovation, and create unnecessary technical barriers to trade. These kinds of measures can pose a particular problem for SMEs, which often do not have the resources to address these problems on their own. USTR is committed to identifying and combating unwarranted technical barriers to U.S. exports, many of which are detailed in this report. USTR's efforts to prevent and remove foreign technical barriers serve the President's goal of doubling U.S. exports by the end of 2014 through the National Export Initiative.

Since the last *TBT Report* was released, the United States has launched new initiatives to promote greater international cooperation among regulatory authorities, trade officials, and standards experts to prevent the emergence of unjustifiable barriers to U.S. exports. We have made progress, for example, in encouraging our trading partners to address unwarranted or burdensome technical regulations through the U.S.-EU High-Level Regulatory Cooperation Forum, the U.S.-Mexico High-Level Regulatory Cooperation Council, the U.S.-Canada Regulatory Cooperation Council, and other fora. We have also taken successful steps to eliminate or reduce specific foreign barriers to U.S. exports, such as Indonesia's rules limiting U.S. poultry and meat imports and Mexico's nutrition labeling requirements that impeded exports of American pre-packaged foods, among others.

This year, USTR will continue to work with other agencies of the U.S. Government, as well as interested stakeholders, to encourage U.S. trading partners to remove their unwarranted or overly burdensome technical barriers. As always, we will engage all available bilateral, regional, and multilateral contexts in our efforts to dismantle unjustifiable barriers to safe, high-quality U.S. industrial, consumer, and agricultural exports and strengthen the rules-based trading system. For example, in our capacity as host of the Asia Pacific Economic Cooperation (APEC) forum in 2011, the United States has made cross-border regulatory cooperation and convergence a top priority for action. We look forward to making further progress on behalf of American manufacturers, workers, farmers, ranchers, and service providers, as well as families who depend on trade-supported American jobs.

Ambassador Ron Kirk
U.S. Trade Representative
March 2011

II.   Executive Summary

The *2011 Report on Technical Barriers to Trade (TBT Report)* is a specialized report focused on significant foreign trade barriers in the form of product standards, technical regulations and testing, certification, and other procedures involved in determining whether products conform to standards and technical regulations.   These standards-related trade measures, known in World Trade Organization (WTO) parlance as "technical barriers to trade," play a critical role in shaping the flow of global trade.

Standards-related measures serve an important function in facilitating global trade, including by enabling greater access to international markets by small- and medium-sized enterprises (SMEs).   Standards-related measures also enable governments to pursue legitimate objectives such as protecting human health and the environment and preventing deceptive practices.   But standards-related measures that are non-transparent, discriminatory, or otherwise unwarranted can act as significant barriers to U.S. trade.   These kinds of measures can pose a particular problem for SMEs, which often do not have the resources to address these problems on their own.

This report is intended to describe and advance U.S. efforts to identify and eliminate such barriers. The opening sections of this report present an overview of technical barriers to trade and the U.S. and international mechanisms for addressing them.[1]   Section II provides an introduction to standards-related measures, including the genesis of this report and the growing importance of standards-related measures in global trade.   Section III provides an overview of standards-related trade obligations, in particular rules governing standards-related measures under the WTO Agreement on Technical Barriers to Trade (TBT Agreement) and U.S. free trade agreements.

Section IV describes the U.S. legal framework for implementing its standards-related trade obligations.   Section V elaborates on standards, including the role of international standards in facilitating trade and fulfilling legitimate public policy objectives and federal agencies' participation in standards development.   Section VI elaborates on conformity assessment procedures, including federal agencies' use of conformity assessment and the possibility for international systems of conformity assessment to facilitate trade.   Section VII describes how the U.S. government identifies technical barriers to trade and the process of interagency and stakeholder consultation it employs to determine how to address them.

Section VIII explains how the United States engages with its trading partners to address standards-related measures that act as barriers and prevent their creation through multilateral, regional, and bilateral channels, including the WTO's Committee on Technical Barriers to Trade (TBT Committee) and cooperative activities under the APEC Subcommittee on Standards and

---

[1] For readers seeking a deeper understanding of the specific topics covered in this report, references and hyperlinks to additional information are provided throughout the report. To access official documents of the WTO (such as those identified by the document symbol "G/TBT/…") click on "simple search" and enter the document symbol at the WTO's document retrieval website: *http://docsonline.wto.org/gen_search.asp?searchmode=simple*

Conformance, among others. Section IX summarizes current trends relating to standards-related measures.

Finally, Section X identifies and describes significant standards-related trade barriers currently facing U.S. producers, along with U.S. government initiatives to eliminate or reduce the impact of these barriers. The report identifies TBT measures in 17 countries – Argentina, Brazil, China, Colombia, India, Indonesia, Japan, Korea, Malaysia, Mexico, Russia, Saudi Arabia, South Africa, Taiwan, Thailand, Turkey, and Vietnam – as well as the European Union (EU) and its 27 Member States.

III. Introduction

Genesis of this Report

Shortly after taking office in 2009, President Obama reaffirmed America's commitment to ensuring the effective implementation and enforcement of the WTO's system of multilateral trading rules. The President's 2009 Trade Policy Agenda vowed an aggressive and transparent program of defending U.S. rights and benefits under the rules-based trading system as a key element in his vision to restore trade's role in leading economic growth and promoting higher living standards. The President's Agenda also recognized that non-tariff barriers have grown in significance for U.S. exporters seeking access to foreign markets. The President reiterated this focus on non-tariff measures in both the 2010 and 2011 Trade Policy Agendas. Two kinds of non-tariff measures in particular pose a particular challenge to U.S. exports: sanitary and phytosanitary (SPS) measures and standards-related measures, also known as "technical barriers to trade" (TBT).

In 2009, Ambassador Kirk called for intensified monitoring of trading partners' non-tariff measures that act as obstacles to U.S. trade. He also vowed increased engagement to resolve trade issues and to help ensure that U.S. trading partners are complying with trade rules – particularly those rules under the WTO agreements concerning SPS and standards-related measures: the Agreement on the Application of Sanitary and Phytosanitary Measures (SPS Agreement) and the TBT Agreement. The goal of this intensified monitoring and engagement is to help to facilitate and expand trade in safe, high-quality U.S. products.

Ambassador Kirk directed that USTR's annual reports be used to bring new energy to the process of identifying non-tariff measures that act as significant barriers to U.S. exports; to provide a central focus for intensified engagement by U.S. agencies in resolving trade concerns related to non-tariff barriers; and to document the actions underway to give greater transparency and confidence to American workers, producers, businesses, and other stakeholders regarding the actions this Administration is taking on their behalf. As such, Ambassador Kirk directed USTR to create a new *Report on Sanitary and Phytosanitary Measures (SPS Report)* and a *Report on Technical Barriers to Trade (TBT Report)*. The *TBT Report* is a specialized report dedicated to significant foreign barriers in the form of product standards, technical regulations, and conformity assessment procedures (standards-related measures). Previously, standards-related measures were addressed by the *National Trade Estimate Report on Foreign Trade Barriers (NTE Report)*.[2]

---

[2] In accordance with section 181 of the Trade Act of 1974 (the 1974 Trade Act), as amended by section 303 of the Trade and Tariff Act of 1984 (the 1984 Trade Act), section 1304 of the Omnibus Trade and Competitiveness Act of 1988 (the 1988 Trade Act), section 311 of the Uruguay Round Trade Agreements Act (1994 Trade Act), and section 1202 of the Internet Tax Freedom Act, the Office of the U.S. Trade Representative is required to submit to the President, the Senate Finance Committee, and appropriate committees in the House of Representatives, an annual report on significant foreign trade barriers. The statute requires an inventory of the most important foreign barriers affecting U.S. exports of goods and services, foreign direct investment by U.S. persons, and protection of intellectual property rights.

The *2011 Report on Technical Barriers to Trade* reflects the President's continuing commitment to reduce or eliminate barriers to U.S. exports, a commitment which was reaffirmed in the President's 2011 Trade Policy Agenda and embodied by the National Export Initiative (NEI), an Administration initiative to double U.S. exports by 2014. By addressing significant foreign trade barriers in the form of standards-related measures, the *TBT Report* meets the requirements under Section 181 of the Trade Act of 1974, as amended, to report on significant foreign trade barriers with respect to standards-related measures. A separate report addressing significant foreign trade barriers in the form of SPS measures (*2011 Report on Sanitary and Phytosanitary Measures*) is being released in parallel to this report.

The *TBT Report* includes country reports that identify specific standards-related trade barriers. The report also includes general information on standards-related measures, the processes and procedures the United States uses to implement these measures domestically, and the tools the United States uses to address standards-related measures when they act as unnecessary barriers to trade. This general information is provided to assist the reader in understanding the issues and trade concerns described in the last two sections of the report, as well as the channels for resolving them. These last two sections review current trends relating to standards-related measures that can have a significant impact on trade and identify and describe significant standards-related trade barriers currently facing U.S. producers and businesses, along with U.S. government initiatives to eliminate or reduce these barriers.

Like the *NTE Report,* the source of the information for the *TBT Report* includes stakeholder comments that USTR solicited through a *Federal Register* notice, reports from U.S. embassies abroad and from other Federal agencies, and USTR's ongoing consultations with domestic stakeholders and trading partners. An appendix to this report includes a list of commenters that submitted comments in response to the *Federal Register* notice.

Central Focus in 2010

During 2010, the United States succeeded in prompting its trading partners to reduce or eliminate a variety of trade restrictive technical barriers identified in last year's report. The United States also stepped up its efforts to help other governments to avoid imposing unnecessary standards-related measures, particularly with respect to innovative technologies and new areas of regulation, and assist them in strengthening their capacity building to promote good regulatory practices. In 2010, the United States also proposed new initiatives in key trade and economic forums, including in the WTO, in negotiations to conclude a broad-based Trans-Pacific Partnership (TPP) agreement, and in APEC, to encourage governments to eliminate and prevent unnecessary technical barriers to trade.

Overview of Standards-Related Measures

Today, standards-related measures play a critical role in shaping the flow of global trade. While tariffs still constitute an important source of distortions and economic costs, the relative role of tariffs in shaping global trade has declined due in large part to successful "rounds" of multilateral tariff reductions in the WTO and its predecessor, the General Agreement on Tariffs and Trade (GATT). Broadly speaking, standards-related measures are documents and procedures that set out specific technical or other requirements for products or processes as well as procedures to ensure that these requirements are met. Standards-related measures have gained prominence in international trade because of a desire to:

- ensure the connectivity and compatibility of inputs sourced in global markets;

- manage the flow of product-related information through complex and increasingly global supply chains;

- organize manufacturing or other production processes around replicable routines and procedures to yield greater product quality assurance;

- meet important regulatory and societal objectives, such as ensuring product safety, preventing deceptive practices, and protecting the environment; and

- promote more environmentally-sound or socially-conscious production methods.

Standards-related measures also play a vital role in enabling greater competition by helping ensure that producers and consumers can purchase components and end products from a wide variety of suppliers. These measures also enable more widespread access to technical innovations. Standards-related measures can offer particularly pronounced benefits to SMEs from this perspective. By establishing a common set of technical requirements that producers can rely on in manufacturing components and end products, uniform standards and product testing procedures can facilitate the diffusion of technology and innovation, contribute to increasing buyer-seller confidence, and assist SMEs to participate in global supply chains.

But when outdated, overly burdensome, discriminatory, or otherwise inappropriate standards-related measures are used, they can reduce competition, stifle innovation, and create unnecessary obstacles to trade. Even when standards-related measures are used appropriately, firms – particularly SMEs – can face significant challenges in accessing information about, and complying with, diverse and evolving technical requirements in major export markets. This is particularly the case when technical requirements change rapidly or differ markedly across markets.

Standards-related measures can be an effective and efficient means of achieving legitimate commercial and policy objectives. For policy makers, industry officials, and other stakeholders, the basic question is: how do we ensure that standards-related measures facilitate innovation, competition, consumer and environmental protection, and other public policy objectives – without creating unnecessary obstacles to trade? As supply chains grow increasingly complex, governments and other stakeholders must also address the question of how to better align standards and technical requirements across jurisdictions and markets to help producers comply with those requirements, and help goods flow across borders.

The rules, procedures, and opportunities for engagement that international, regional, and bilateral trade agreements establish serve as an important foundation for addressing many of these questions. The TBT Agreement is the principal agreement establishing multilateral rules governing standards-related measures. (Box 1 lays out definitions provided under the TBT Agreement for standards-related measures.) U.S. free trade agreements (FTAs) establish additional rules on these measures with specific trading partners. The TBT Agreement's rules are vital in setting the terms on which the United States engages with its trading partners on standards-related measures, and U.S. FTAs build on these rules in important ways. These agreements are described in more detail in Section III below.

A broad and active agenda of U.S. engagement on many fronts is needed to ensure that foreign standards-related measures do not impose unwarranted barriers to trade. USTR leads Federal government policy deliberations on these measures through the interagency Trade Policy Staff Committee (TPSC). U.S. activities in the WTO are at the forefront of USTR's efforts to prevent and resolve trade concerns arising from standards-related measures. Coordinating with relevant agencies through the TPSC, USTR engages with other governments in many venues, including those established by U.S. FTAs and through regional and multilateral organizations, such as the WTO, APEC and the Organization for Economic Cooperation and Development (OECD). USTR also raises standards-related issues in bilateral dialogues with U.S. trading partners. These efforts are designed to ensure that U.S. trading partners adhere to internationally-agreed rules governing these measures and to reduce or eliminate unnecessary measures of this kind that can create barriers for U.S. producers and businesses.

Box 1. Key Definitions in the WTO Agreement on Technical Barriers to Trade

Technical regulation

> Document which lays down product characteristics or their related processes and production methods, including the applicable administrative provisions, with which compliance is mandatory. It may also include or deal exclusively with terminology, symbols, packaging, marking, or labeling requirements as they apply to a product, process, or production method.

Standard

> Document approved by a recognized body, that provides, for common and repeated use, rules, guidelines, or characteristics for products or related processes and production methods, with which compliance is not mandatory. It may also include or deal exclusively with terminology, symbols, packaging, marking, or labeling requirements as they apply to a product, process, or production method.

Conformity assessment procedures

> Any procedure used, directly or indirectly, to determine that relevant requirements in technical regulations or standards are fulfilled.

> *Explanatory note:* Conformity assessment procedures include, *inter alia*, procedures for sampling, testing and inspection; evaluation, verification and assurance of conformity; registration, accreditation, and approval as well as their combinations.

Source: Annex 1 of the TBT Agreement.

Note: These definitions apply only with respect to products and related processes and production methods, not to services.

IV.   Overview of Trade Obligations on Standards-Related Measures

TBT Agreement

The TBT Agreement is designed to ensure that standards-related measures serve legitimate objectives, are transparent, and do not create unnecessary obstacles to trade.   The TBT Agreement contains a comprehensive set of obligations for WTO Members on the development and use of these measures.   It establishes rules on developing, adopting, and applying voluntary product standards and mandatory technical regulations – as well as for the conformity assessment procedures (such as testing or certification) used to determine whether a particular product meets such standards or regulations.   These rules help distinguish legitimate standards-related measures from protectionist measures, and ensure that testing and other conformity assessment procedures are fair and reasonable.

The TBT Agreement recognizes that WTO Members have the right to take standards-related measures necessary to protect human health, safety and the environment at the levels they consider appropriate and to achieve other legitimate objectives.   At the same time, the TBT Agreement imposes a series of rules regarding the development and application of those measures.   For example, the TBT Agreement requires governments to develop standards-related measures through transparent processes, and to base these measures on relevant international standards (where effective and appropriate).   The TBT Agreement also prohibits measures that discriminate against imported products or create unnecessary obstacles to trade.   The TBT Agreement sets out a *Code of Good Practice* for both governments and non-governmental standardizing bodies to guide the preparation, adoption, and application of voluntary standards. The Code is open to acceptance by any standardizing body located in the territory of any WTO Member. Box 2 outlines the key disciplines of the TBT Agreement.

Box 2. Key principles and provisions of the TBT Agreement

Non-discrimination: The Agreement states that "in respect of their technical regulations, products imported from the territory of any Member [shall] be accorded treatment no less favorable than that accorded to like products of national origin and to like products originating in any other country." (Art. 2.1) The Agreement requires Members to ensure that "conformity assessment procedures are prepared, adopted and applied so as to grant TBT Agreement access for suppliers of like products originating in the territories of other Members under conditions no less favorable than those accorded to suppliers of like products of national origin or originating in any other country, in a comparable situation." (Art. 5.1.1) The Agreement also requires that Members ensure that related fees are equitable (Art. 5.2.5) and that they respect the confidentiality of information about the results of conformity assessment procedures for imported products in the same way they do for domestic products. (Art. 5.2.4)

Avoidance of unnecessary obstacles to trade: When preparing or applying a technical regulation, a Member must ensure that the regulation is not more trade-restrictive than necessary to fulfill the Member's legitimate objective. (Art. 2.2) The obligation to avoid unnecessary obstacles to trade applies also to conformity assessment procedures. They must not be stricter than necessary to provide adequate confidence that products conform with applicable requirements. (Art. 5.1.2)

Better alignment of technical regulations, standards, and conformity assessment procedures: The Agreement calls on Members to use relevant international standards, or the relevant parts of them, as a basis for their technical regulations and to use relevant international recommendations and guides, or relevant portions of them, as the basis

9

for their conformity assessment procedures. The Agreement, however, does not require the use of relevant international standards, guides and recommendations if they would be ineffective or inappropriate to fulfill the Member's "legitimate objectives." (Arts. 2.4 and 5.4) In addition, Members should participate "within the limits of their resources" in the preparation by international standardization bodies, of international standards for products for which they either have adopted, or expect to adopt, technical regulation, and in the elaboration of international guides and recommendations for conformity assessment procedures. (Art.2.6 and 5.5)

Use of performance-based requirements: Whenever appropriate, product requirements should be set in terms of *performance* rather than design or descriptive characteristics. (Art. 2.8)

International systems of conformity assessment: Members shall, whenever practicable, formulate and adopt international systems for conformity assessment and become members thereof or participate therein. (Art. 9.1)

Acceptance of technical regulations as equivalent: Alongside harmonization, the Agreement encourages Members to accept technical regulations that other Members adopt as "equivalent" to their own if these regulations adequately fulfill the objectives of their own regulations. (Art. 2.7)

Mutual recognition of conformity assessment: The Agreement requires each Member to recognize "whenever possible" the results of conformity assessment procedures (*e.g.* test results or certifications), provided the Member is satisfied that those procedures offer an assurance of conformity that is equivalent as its own. (Art. 6.1) (Without such recognition, products might have to be tested twice, first by the exporting country and then by the importing country.) The Agreement recognizes that Members may need to consult in advance to arrive at a "mutually satisfactory understanding" regarding the competences of their respective conformity assessment bodies. (Art. 6.1) The Agreement also encourages Members to enter into negotiations to conclude agreements providing for the mutual recognition of each other's conformity assessment results (*i.e.,* mutual recognition agreements or MRAs). (Art. 6.3)

Transparency: To help ensure transparency, the Agreement requires Members to publish a notice at an early stage and notify other Members through the WTO Secretariat when it proposes to adopt a technical regulation or conformity assessment procedure and to include in the notification a brief indication of the purpose of the proposed measure. These obligations apply whenever a relevant international standard, guide, or recommendation does not exist or the technical content of a proposed technical regulation or conformity assessment procedure is not in accordance with the technical content of relevant international standards, guides, or recommendations. In such circumstances, Members must allow "reasonable time" for other Members to comment on proposed technical regulations and conformity assessment procedures, which the TBT Committee has recommended to be "at least 60 days" (G/TBT/26), and take comments it receives from other Members into account. (Art. 2.9 and 5.6) The Agreement establishes a Code of Good Practice that is applicable to voluntary standards and obligates Members and standardizing bodies that have accepted it to publish every six months a work program containing the standards it is currently preparing and give interested parties at least 60 days to comment on a draft standard; once the standard is adopted it must be promptly published. (Annex 3) The Agreement also requires that all technical regulations and conformity assessment procedures be promptly published. (Art. 2.11 and 5.8) In addition, the Agreement requires each Member to establish an inquiry point to answer all reasonable questions from other Members and interested parties and to provide documents relating to technical regulations, standards, and conformity assessment procedures adopted or proposed within its territory. (Art. 10.1)

Technical assistance: The Agreement calls on Members to provide technical assistance to other Members. (Art. 11) Technical assistance can be provided to help developing country Members with such matters as preparing technical regulations, establishing national standardizing bodies, participating in international standardization bodies, and establishing bodies to assess conformity with technical regulations.

Enforcement and dispute settlement: The Agreement establishes the *Committee on Technical Barriers to Trade* as the major forum for WTO Members to consult on matters relating to the operation of the Agreement, including specific trade concerns about measures that Members have proposed or adopted. (Art. 13) The TBT Agreement provides for disputes under the Agreement to be resolved under the auspices of the WTO Dispute Settlement Body and in accordance with the terms of the WTO's Dispute Settlement Understanding. (Art. 14)

Other: As noted above, the Agreement sets out a "Code of Good Practice" for preparing, adopting, and applying voluntary standards. (Annex 3) Standardizing bodies that Members establish at the central level of government must comply with the Code and Members must take reasonable measures to ensure that local government and private sector standardizing bodies within their territories also accept and comply with the Code. (Art. 4.1) The Code is open to acceptance by any standardizing body in the territory of a WTO Member, including private sector bodies as well as public sector bodies. The Code requires Members and other standardizing bodies that have accepted it to adhere to obligations similar to those for technical regulations, for example, to ensure that the standards they adopt do not create unnecessary obstacles to trade and are based on relevant international standards, except where ineffective or inappropriate.

Note: The OECD and WTO have also developed summaries of the TBT Agreement. See Trade Policy Working Paper No. 58, *Do Bilateral and Regional Approaches for Reducing Technical Barriers to Trade Converge Towards The Multilateral Trading System?* (OECD (TAD/TC/WP(2007)12/FINAL), WTO Trade Gateway, and TBT Committee reports and recommendations.

Access to information on product-related technical requirements is critical for facilitating trade. Producers, growers, manufacturers, and other supply chain participants need to know the requirements with which their products must comply in order to sell them in prospective markets. The TBT Agreement, therefore, requires every WTO Member to establish a national Inquiry Point that is able to answer reasonable questions from other Members and interested parties concerning its proposed or existing measures, and provide relevant documents, as appropriate. It also requires each WTO Member to ensure all standards-related measures that it adopts are promptly published or otherwise made publicly available.

The TBT Agreement requires WTO Members to provide other Members the opportunity to participate in the development of mandatory standards-related measures, which helps to ensure that standards-related measures do not become unnecessary obstacles to trade.[3] In particular, the TBT Agreement requires each Member to publish a notice in advance that it proposes to adopt a technical regulation or conformity assessment procedure.[4] It also requires each WTO Member to notify proposed technical regulations and conformity assessment procedures to the WTO so that other WTO Members may comment on them in writing. WTO Members are required, without discrimination, to take into account these written comments, plus the results of any requested discussions of those comments, when finalizing their measures.[5] In 2010 alone, WTO Members notified 1,419 new or amended technical regulations and conformity assessment procedures to the WTO. Box 3 shows the growth in notifications since 1995.[6]

---

[3] Depending on the WTO Member's domestic processes, interested parties may participate directly in that Member's process for developing new standards-related measures, for example, by submitting written comments to the Member, or indirectly by working with their own governments to submit comments.

[4] Members typically do this by publishing a notice in an official journal of national circulation or on a government website that they propose to adopt a technical regulation or conformity assessment procedure or by publishing the full text of the draft measure.

[5] The obligations described in this paragraph apply to measures that have a significant effect on trade and are not based on relevant international standards, guides, or recommendations or in circumstances where relevant international standards, guides, or recommendations do not exist. In many instances, however, Members, including the United States, notify proposed technical regulations and conformity assessment procedures regardless of whether they are based on relevant international standards.

[6] WTO Members notify new measures, as well as addenda and corrigenda to previously notified measures. An addendum alerts WTO Members that substantive or technical changes have been made to a measure that has been previously notified. A corrigendum conveys editorial or administrative corrections to a previous notification.

Box 3: Number of TBT Notifications to the WTO (Source: WTO, G/TBT/29)

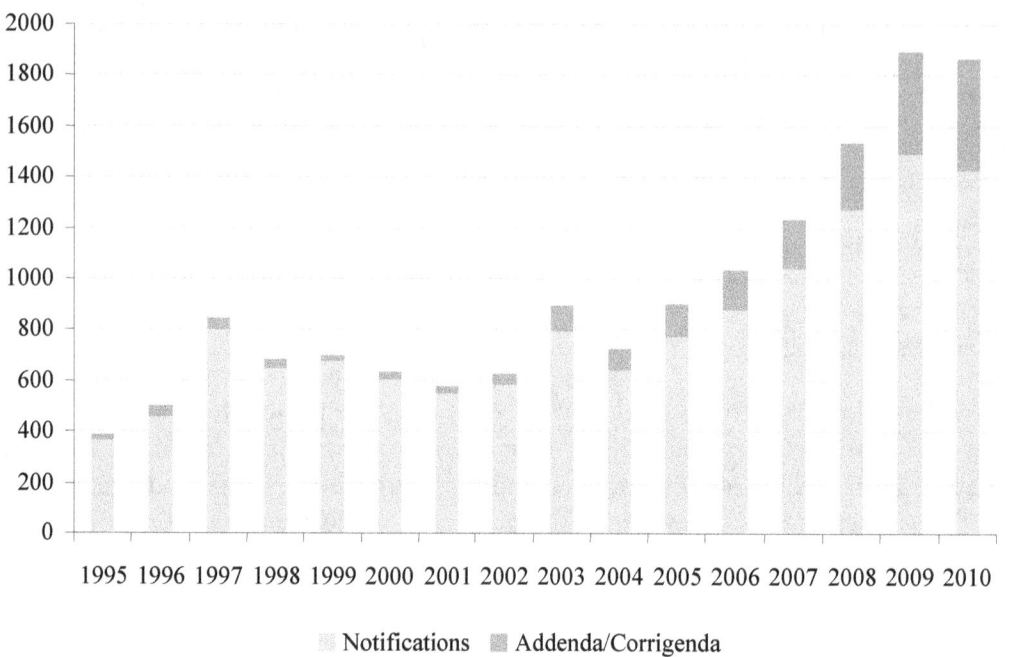

Notifications   Addenda/Corrigenda

Article 13 of the TBT Agreement establishes a "Committee on Technical Barriers to Trade" to oversee the operation and implementation of the TBT Agreement. The TBT Committee is open to participation by all 153 WTO Members. The TBT Committee is one of over a dozen standing bodies (others include the Committees on Import Licensing, Antidumping Practices, and Rules of Origin, for example) that report to the WTO Council for Trade in Goods. The activities of the TBT Committee are described in detail below.

Operation of the TBT Agreement

The TBT Agreement seeks to set out simple rules covering complex requirements developed and implemented by disparate bodies (central and local governmental agencies; inter-governmental entities; and non-governmental, national and international standardizing organizations). WTO Members' central government authorities have primary responsibility for ensuring compliance with the TBT Agreement, including by taking reasonable measures to ensure that local and non-governmental bodies, such as private sector standards developing organizations, adhere to the relevant provisions. Further, each Member must inform the TBT Committee of the laws, policies, and procedures it has adopted to implement and administer the TBT Agreement.[7]

Many Members also notify adopted technical regulations and conformity assessment procedures (regardless of whether or not they are based on relevant international standards).

[7] See G/TBT/GEN/1/Rev.8 for a list of Members' submissions on the measures they have taken to implement and administer the TBT Agreement.

The quality and coherence of these laws, policies, and procedures – as well as how they are put into practice – influence the extent to which standards-related measures in any particular country are transparent, non-discriminatory, and avoid creating unnecessary obstacles to trade, as the TBT Agreement requires. In practice, sound mechanisms for internal coordination among a Member's trade, regulatory, and standards officials are critical to ensuring the Member effectively implements the TBT Agreement. When interested agencies and officials coordinate their efforts in developing standards-related measures, it makes it more likely that the government will consider alternative technical specifications that may lessen any potential adverse effects on trade.

Further, when governments take account of how the products they propose to regulate are traded in global markets, it can make the measures they adopt more effective in fulfilling the objective of the regulation. The effectiveness of a WTO Member's internal coordination also often determines the extent to which it is able to resolve specific trade concerns raised by other Members. In some developing countries, ineffective internal coordination and a lack of established procedures for developing standards-related measures are a key concern. For these countries, technical assistance or cooperative efforts to improve internal coordination can be vital in helping U.S. exporters sell into these markets.

In discharging its responsibility in overseeing the TBT Agreement, the TBT Committee conducts triennial reviews of systemic issues affecting WTO Members' policies and procedures for implementing specific obligations.[8] In the course of these reviews, Members adopt specific recommendations and decisions, and lay out a forward-looking work program to strengthen the implementation and operation of the TBT Agreement. To advance their understanding of systemic issues, Members share experiences and participate in special events and regional workshops to explore topics in depth. Recent Committee events have covered Good Regulatory Practice, Conformity Assessment, and the Role of International Standards in Economic Development. The Committee held the 6th Special Meeting on Information Exchange, in June 2010, and plans to host a Workshop on Regulatory Cooperation in November 2011.

In addition to its triennial reviews and the related special events and workshops, the TBT Committee meets three times a year. At these meetings, Members may raise any specific trade concern regarding standards-related measures that other Members have proposed or adopted. The Committee's discussion of these concerns can help to clarify the technical aspects of the measures concerned, promote greater understanding of how the measures might affect trade, and perhaps even help to resolve the concerns. In 2010, WTO Members raised 61 specific trade concerns in the TBT Committee, including, for example, concerns regarding measures relating to managing hazards arising from use of chemicals, labeling and other non-safety requirements relating to food products, and duplicative or redundant testing requirements on a wide variety of goods such as toys and medical devices. WTO Members have underscored the importance of the Committee's regular discussions of specific trade concerns, and agreed that the Committee's work has helped to clarify and resolve trade issues between WTO Members.[9]

---

[8] The results of the most recent triennial review are discussed in Section V.

[9] See the discussion of the Operation of the Committee in the "*Fifth Triennial Review of the Operation and Implementation of the Agreement on Technical Barriers to Trade under Article 15.4*" G/TBT/26.

Box 4 shows the number of specific trade concerns WTO Members have raised in the TBT Committee since 1995. The general rise in concerns raised over the past few years reflects several factors – including an increase in the number of proposed measures that WTO Members have notified to the WTO, a heightened focus on standards-related activities, increased concern that these measures may be used as a form of disguised protectionism, and an increasing perception that discussions in the TBT Committee, as well as bilateral discussions on the margins of Committee meetings, can lead to results in addressing trade concerns. For a full accounting of the concerns raised in the Committee since 1995, see G/TBT/28.

Box 4: Number of specific trade concerns raised per year in the TBT Committee (Source: WTO, G/TBT/29)

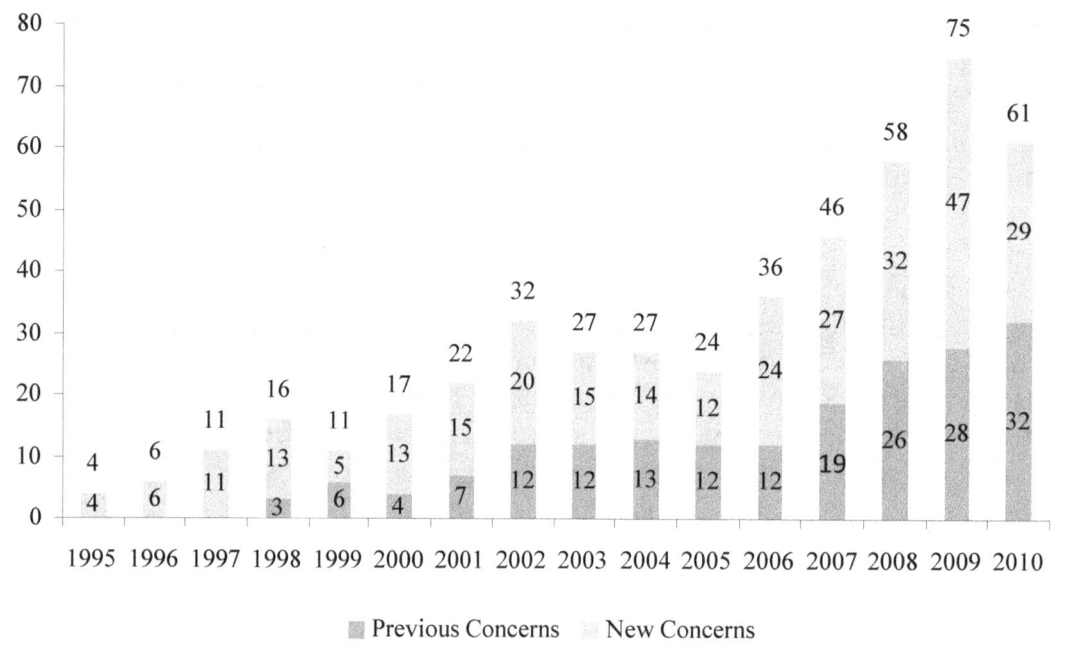

Standards-Related Provisions in U.S. Free Trade Agreements[10]

In U.S. FTAs, the parties reaffirm their commitment to the TBT Agreement, and agree to strengthen its key provisions. U.S. FTAs build on the disciplines in the TBT Agreement in important ways, including by providing for greater transparency, establishing mechanisms for more in-depth consultation on specific trade concerns, and facilitating cooperation and coordination with FTA partners on systemic issues. As a result, the U.S. approach to standards-related measures in its FTAs is commonly referred to as "TBT plus."[11] U.S. FTAs, for example,

---

[10] This section describes TBT provisions of U.S. FTAs with Australia, Bahrain, Central America and the Dominican Republic, Chile, Morocco, Oman, and Peru, all concluded in 2003 or later. Pending FTAs with Panama, Korea, and Colombia contain similar TBT provisions. In addition to these FTAs, the NAFTA also includes provisions that go beyond those contained in the TBT Agreement, for example, with respect to transparency, cooperation with trading partners regarding standards-related measures, and national treatment for testing and certification bodies. The U.S. FTA with Singapore also includes TBT provisions that seek to enhance the parties' cooperation on standards-related measures.

[11] For a discussion of agreements that promote divergence from multilateral approaches (or "TBT minus") see

require governments to publish the full text of their proposed standards-related measures, rather than simply publish a notice that it proposes to adopt the measure. In addition, U.S. FTAs provide interested parties, as well governments, the opportunity to comment on proposed measures. These provisions enable the United States and other FTA partners to engage and monitor each other's proposed measures more closely.

U.S. FTAs also contain substantive obligations that go beyond those in the TBT Agreement. For example, U.S. FTAs require FTA partners to accredit or otherwise recognize U.S. testing and certification bodies under no less favorable terms than FTA partners accord their own testing and certification bodies. Recent U.S. FTAs, as well as the earlier NAFTA, also build in mechanisms (such as special committees) for closer and more enduring engagement and cooperation on standards-related measures. These mechanisms can prevent specific trade concerns from arising and assist the FTA governments in resolving emerging problems.

By enhancing understanding of each Party's respective rulemaking processes and standards and conformance infrastructure, these consultative mechanisms can enable early identification of potential trade problems and provide opportunities for the FTA partners to discuss technical alternatives before a measure is finalized.[12] The provisions in U.S. FTAs that provide for more timely and robust consultations, enhance the notifications process, and provide for direct bilateral engagement on notified measures are particularly important in this regard.

Like the TBT Agreement, the TBT provisions of U.S. FTAs recognize that FTA partners should not be prevented from taking measures necessary to protect public health and safety or the environment. At the same time, U.S. FTAs lay out ways in which FTA partners can reduce the impact on their bilateral trade stemming from differing regulatory regimes. Several U.S. FTAs also contain provisions designed to encourage FTA partners to accept each other's regulations as equivalent to their own, where appropriate.

Lastly, recent U.S. FTAs provide strong support for the *U.S. Standards Strategy* – which establishes a framework for developing voluntary product standards – by formally recognizing the TBT Committee's *2000 Decision on Principles for the Development of International Standards.*[13] The U.S. experience with the *2000 Committee Decision* is described at length in G/TBT/W/305. These issues are discussed in more detail in Section V below.

Trade Policy Working Paper No. 58, *Do Bilateral and Regional Approaches for Reducing Technical Barriers to Trade Converge Towards The Multilateral Trading System?* (OECD (TAD/TC/WP(2007)12/FINAL).

[12] See, for example, G/TBT/W/317 for a discussion of the cooperative standards-related work on automobiles, chemicals, food, energy, and other issues under the NAFTA.

[13] Decision on Principles for the Development of International Standards, Guides and Recommendations with Relation to Articles 2, 5 and Annex 3 of the TBT Agreement, contained in document G/TBT/1/Rev.9, Part I, Section III (pp. 10-12) and Annex B (pp. 37-39).

Box 5: Key Standards-Related Provisions in U.S. Free Trade Agreements

The United States has concluded FTAs with a number of countries. While each agreement is unique, many of these free trade agreements share common provisions relating to standards-related measures. This box summarizes standards-related provisions common to U.S. FTAs with Australia, Bahrain, Central America and the Dominican Republic, Chile, Morocco, Oman, and Peru. Pending FTAs with Panama, Korea, and Colombia contain these provisions as well.

Affirmation of the TBT Agreement: The FTAs reaffirm the parties' obligations under the TBT Agreement and use the TBT Agreement's definitions of key terms, such as technical regulation, standard, and conformity assessment procedures.

International standards: The FTAs require FTA partners to apply the principles of the *2000 Committee Decision* in determining whether an international standard, guide, or recommendation exists.

Conformity assessment procedures: The FTAs recognize the variety of mechanisms that exist for facilitating acceptance of each other's conformity assessment procedures, and they list specific examples of those mechanisms. The agreements also call for FTA partners to intensify their exchange of information regarding these mechanisms; require an FTA partner to explain when it will not accept, or negotiate agreements to accept, another partner's conformity assessment results; call for FTA partners to recognize conformity assessment bodies in another partner's territory on a national treatment basis; and require FTA partners to explain any refusal to recognize another party's conformity assessment body.

Transparency: The FTAs state that each party shall permit persons from the other party to participate in the development of standards-related measures on terms no less favorable than those it accords to its own persons. They also enhance TBT Agreement transparency provisions by requiring that proposals be notified directly to the other Party; that objectives be included when notifying proposals; that interested parties as well as the FTA partner be provided a meaningful opportunity to comment and to have their comments taken into account in finalizing the measure; that 60 days be allowed for comment; that proposals be published or otherwise made available; that responses be provided to significant comments received at the time a final measure is published; and that additional information be provided about the objectives when requested.

Cooperation: The FTAs provide for FTA partners to intensify their joint work on technical regulations, standards, and conformity assessment bodies. They also urge participating governments to identify bilateral initiatives for specific issues or sectors.

Information Exchange: The FTAs call on each FTA partner to provide information or explanations regarding proposed measures within a reasonable period following a request from another FTA partner.

Administration: Each FTA creates its own committee or subcommittee to monitor application of the agreement's provisions, address specific issues that arise under the agreement, enhance cooperation, and exchange information on pertinent developments.

Note: For more information, see http://www.ustr.gov/trade-agreements/free-trade-agreements.

V. U.S. Statutory and Administrative Framework for Implementing Standards-Related Trade Obligations

The United States maintains a robust system to support implementation of its trade obligations on standards-related measures through strong central management of its regulatory regime, an effective interagency trade policy mechanism, and public consultation. The legal framework for implementing U.S. obligations under the TBT Agreement and standards-related provisions in U.S. FTAs includes the _Administrative Procedure Act of 1946_ (APA), and the _Trade Agreements Act of 1979_ (TAA).[14] The APA establishes a process of public participation in rulemakings by U.S. agencies through a system of notice and comment. The TAA prohibits Federal agencies from engaging in any standards-related activity that creates unnecessary obstacles to trade and directs them to consider the use of international standards in rulemaking.

The TAA establishes USTR as the lead agency within the Federal government for coordinating and developing international trade policy related to standards-related activities, as well as in discussions and negotiations with foreign countries on standards-related matters. In carrying out this responsibility, USTR is required to inform and consult with Federal agencies having expertise in the matters under discussion and negotiation. The TAA also directs the Secretaries of Commerce and Agriculture to keep abreast of international standards activities, to identify those activities that may substantially affect U.S. commerce, and to inform, consult, and coordinate with USTR with respect to international standards-related activities.

The APA provides the foundation for transparency and accountability in developing Federal regulations. The APA requires agencies to undertake a notice and comment process open to all members of the public, both foreign and domestic, for all rulemakings, and to take these comments into account in the final rule.[15] In accordance with the APA, agencies publish proposed technical regulations and conformity assessment procedures and solicit public comment in the _Federal Register_. To fulfill WTO obligations to notify proposed technical regulations and conformity assessment procedures, the National Institute of Standards and Technology (NIST) in the Department of Commerce serves as the U.S. notification authority. NIST officials review the _Federal Register_ and other materials on a daily basis and notify the WTO of technical regulations and conformity assessment procedures that agencies propose to adopt. NIST also serves as the U.S. Inquiry Point for purposes of the TBT Agreement.

The foundation for central regulatory review is _Executive Order 12866 – Regulatory Planning and Review_ (E.O. 12866) and the implementing guidance of the Office and Management and Budget (OMB) _Circular A-4_. E.O. 12866 lays out the philosophy, principles, and actions that

---

[14] The standards-related provisions of the TAA are codified at United States Code, Title 19, Chapter 13, Subchapter II, Technical Barriers to Trade (Standards).

[15] The term "rule" refers to "an agency statement of general or particular applicability and future effect designed to implement, interpret, or prescribe law or policy...." 5 U.S.C. § 551(4). "Rule making" means the "agency process for formulating, amending, or repealing a rule...." 5 U.S.C. § 551(5). These definitions include rules or rulemakings regarding technical regulations and conformity assessment procedures. The APA makes exceptions for urgent matters, allowing Federal agencies to omit notice and comment, for example, where they find that notice and public procedures are impracticable or contrary to the public interest. 5 U.S.C. § 553(b)(3).

guide federal agencies in planning, developing, and reviewing Federal regulations. E.O. 12866 and Circular A-4 are the primary basis on which good regulatory practice (GRP) has been integrated into the Federal regulatory structure. These practices ensure openness, transparency, and accountability in the regulatory process, and, as a result, help ensure that the United States fulfills key TBT Agreement and U.S. FTA obligations. GRP,[16] such as that embodied in E.O. 12866 and *OMB Circular A-4,* enables government agencies to achieve their public policy objectives efficiently and effectively. GRP is also critical in reducing the possibility that governments will adopt standards-related measures that create unnecessary obstacles to trade.

Under the procedures spelled out in E.O. 12866, prior to adopting any significant regulatory action (*e.g.,* a proposed technical regulation) federal agencies must submit it for review to OMB. Significant regulatory actions are defined as those with an estimated annual impact on the U.S. economy of at least $100 million. OMB reviews federal agencies' proposed regulatory actions and consults with USTR and other agencies as needed. This review is designed to ensure, *inter alia,* that proposed regulatory actions are not duplicative or inconsistent with other planned or existing Federal regulatory actions, are consistent with U.S. international trade obligations, and take into account the trade impact of proposed regulatory actions. At the conclusion of this process, OMB provides guidance to the pertinent agency to ensure that its regulatory actions are consistent with applicable law, Presidential priorities, and E.O. 12866's regulatory principles.

On January 18, 2011, President Obama issued *Executive Order 13563 - Improving Regulation and Regulatory Review* (EO 15363), which reaffirmed and supplemented E.O. 12866. E.O. 13563 states that "[the U.S.] regulatory system must protect public health, welfare, safety, and our environment while promoting economic growth, innovation, competitiveness, and job creation....It must allow for public participation and an open exchange of ideas. It must promote predictability and reduce uncertainty. It must identify and use the best, most innovative, and least burdensome tools for achieving regulatory ends. It must take into account benefits and costs, both quantitative and qualitative." E.O. 13563 sets out certain regulatory principles, as well as new requirements designed to promote public participation, improve regulatory integration and innovation, increase flexibility, ensure scientific integrity, and increase retrospective analysis of existing rules.

In addition to the statutes and policies outlined above, the *National Technology Transfer and Advancement Act* (NTTAA) and OMB's implementing guidance to Federal agencies, *OMB Circular A-119,* require Federal agencies to use[17] voluntary consensus standards[18] in their

---

[16] For a discussion of good regulatory practices from the perspective of APEC and the OECD, see:
APEC, "*Information Notes on Good Practice for Technical Regulation,*" September 2000.
OECD, *Cutting Red Tape: National Strategies for Administrative Simplification.* Paris, 2006.
OECD, *Background Document on Oversight Bodies for Regulatory Reform*. Paris: OECD, 2007.
OECD, *Regulatory Impact Analyses: Best Practices in OECD Countries.* Paris: OECD, 1997.
OECD, *Regulatory Performance: Ex post Evaluation of Regulatory Policies*. Paris: OECD, 2003.
OECD and APEC, *APEC-OECD Integrated Checklist on Regulatory Reform.* Mexico City, 2005.

[17] Circular A-119 defines "use" as the inclusion of a standard in whole, in part, or by reference in a regulation.

[18] Circular A-119 states that the following attributes define bodies that develop voluntary consensus standards: openness, balance of interests, due process, an appeals process, and consensus.

regulatory activities wherever possible and to avoid using "government-unique" standards.[19] The purpose is to discourage Federal agencies from developing their own standards where suitable voluntary consensus standards already exist. In addition, voluntary consensus standards can often effectively achieve an agency's regulatory objectives. The NTTAA and the TAA are complementary: The NTTAA directs Federal agencies to look to voluntary consensus standards to meet their regulatory objectives, while the TAA directs them to consider using relevant international standards. As elaborated in Section V, international standards are those that recognized bodies, either intergovernmental or non-governmental, develop in accordance with principles such as openness, transparency, and consensus.

For additional information on the laws, policies, and interagency processes through which the United States implements the TBT Agreement, see G/TBT/2/Add.2, G/TBT/W/285, and G/TBT/W/315. See also the *Report on the Use of Voluntary Standards in Support of Regulation in the United States* presented to the High Level Regulatory Cooperation Forum of the United States – European Union Transatlantic Economic Council (TEC) in October 2009. For additional information on the relationship between technical barriers to trade and GRP, see G/TBT/W/287 and USITC Working Paper No ID-24, *The Role of Good Regulatory Practice in Reducing Technical Barriers to Trade*.

---

[19] Circular A-119 defines "government-unique standards" as standards developed by the government for its own uses.

VI.   Standards

Voluntary standards serve a variety of functions and their use supports world trade, for example by ensuring the connectivity and compatibility of inputs sourced in global markets. The TBT Agreement has a specific definition of "standard" – a document approved by a recognized body that provides, for common and repeated use, rules, guidelines or characteristics for products or related processes and production methods for which compliance is not mandatory. Voluntary standards can facilitate buyer-seller transactions, spur competition[20] and innovation, increase the efficiency of production, unify markets, and promote societal goals. When used as the basis for establishing a technical requirement in a regulation, voluntary standards can help officials harness relevant technology to achieve regulatory goals in a cost effective manner. In the United States, responsibility for developing voluntary standards rests almost exclusively, and appropriately, with the private sector, as this is where the technical know-how for sophisticated products and complex processes resides.[21]

The TBT Agreement acknowledges the diversity of standardizing bodies, and seeks to minimize unnecessary obstacles to trade that can arise from multiple standards for the same product, specifications that favor domestic goods over imported ones, lack of transparency, or dominance by a region or government in standards development. To promote greater harmonization of the technical requirements that WTO Members impose, the TBT Agreement promotes the use of and participation in the development of international standards.

Additionally, the TBT Agreement requires Members to base technical regulations and conformity assessment procedures on relevant international standards, guides and recommendations, except where they would be inappropriate or ineffective in meeting a legitimate objective. The TBT Agreement affords technical regulations based on relevant international standards a rebuttable presumption that they are not unnecessary obstacles to trade under the TBT Agreement. The TBT Agreement also strongly discourages standardizing bodies from developing standards where international standards already exist.

The TBT Agreement does not, however, designate specific standardizing bodies as "international." Instead, in its *2000 Decision on the Principles for the Development of International Standards, Guides and Recommendations (2000 Committee Decision)*, the TBT Committee adopted a set of six principles for developing international standards.[22] The *2000 Committee Decision* is designed to clarify the concept of "international standard" and to advance objectives such as greater harmonization of technical requirements across markets. The six

---

[20] See *Standards & Competitiveness: Coordinating for Results: Removing Standards-Related Trade Barriers Through Effective Collaboration*, International Trade Administration, 2005.

[21] Agriculture is a notable exception. USDA maintains several programs, such as the Agricultural Marketing Service, for the development of voluntary standards on the quality and identity of agricultural products sold in the U.S. market.

[22] Decision on Principles for the Development of International Standards, Guides and Recommendations with Relation to Articles 2, 5 and Annex 3 of the TBT Agreement, contained in document G/TBT/1/Rev.9, Part I, Section III (pp. 10-12) and Annex B (on pp. 37-39).

principles are: (1) openness; (2) transparency; (3) impartiality and consensus; (4) relevance and effectiveness; (5) coherence; and (6) the development dimension.

It is the policy of the U.S. government to use the term "international standard" to refer to those standards developed in conformity with the *2000 Committee Decision* principles.[23] For example, U.S. FTAs require trading partners to apply the *2000 Committee Decision* principles when determining whether a relevant international standard exists. When WTO Members use international standards developed in conformity with the *2000 Committee Decision* in their technical regulations, it can promote greater global regulatory alignment and reduce the adverse trade effects that regulatory divergences can create. Application of principles such as consensus, openness, and transparency when developing standards helps ensure standards are globally relevant and respond to both technical and regulatory needs. The *2000 Committee Decision* also helps ensure that all interested parties, including producers and consumers that may be affected by a particular standard, can participate in developing it.

Annex 3 of the TBT Agreement contains a *Code of Good Practice* for WTO Members and non-governmental standardizing bodies to follow in preparing, adopting, and applying standards. Central government standardizing bodies must adhere to the *Code*. WTO Members are required to take reasonable measures to ensure non-governmental standardizing bodies conform to the *Code* as well. In the United States, the American National Standards Institute (ANSI) has accepted the *Code of Good Practice* on behalf of the over 200 standards developing organizations (SDOs) that ANSI has accredited. ANSI, a private sector body, is the coordinator of the U.S. voluntary standards system with a membership that consists of standards developers, certification bodies, industry, government, and other stakeholders. In coordination with its membership, ANSI developed and implements the *U.S. Standards Strategy*. For more information on the ANSI system, see *Overview of the U.S. Standardization System*.

ANSI accredits SDOs based on its *Essential Requirements*. Many elements of these requirements mirror the *2000 Committee Decision*. The *Essential Requirements* require each SDO to maintain procedures for developing standards that ensure openness, consensus, due process, and participation by materially affected interests. ANSI also serves as the U.S. national standards body member of the International Organization for Standardization (ISO) and the International Electrotechnical Commission (IEC). Federal agency representatives participate actively in ANSI policy forums, as well as in the technical committees of ANSI-accredited SDOs, on an equal basis as other ANSI members.

OMB Circular A-119 contains guidance for Federal agencies in participating in the development of voluntary standards. *Circular A-119* directs Federal agencies to participate in private sector standards developing organizations consistent with agency missions and priorities. The Interagency Committee for Standards Policy, which NIST chairs, coordinates implementation of this guidance. More than 4,000 federal agency officials participate in the private sector standards development activities of 497 organizations[24] to support regulatory needs, enable efficient procurement, and to help devise solutions to support emerging national priorities. It is notable, however, that the governments in some regions and countries take a non-technical and

---

[23] The U.S. experience with the *2000 Committee Decision* is described in G/TBT/W/305.

[24] Source: NIST, 2008.

more commanding role in standards setting than federal agencies generally do. For example, some governments direct their national standards bodies or central government bodies to develop voluntary standards to achieve specific regulatory needs.

VII.   Conformity Assessment Procedures

Conformity assessment enables buyers, sellers, consumers, and regulators to have confidence that products sourced in global market meet specific requirements.[25] Governments may mandate conformity assessment procedures – such as testing, sampling, and certification requirements – to ensure that the requirements they have established in standards or regulations for a product, process, system, person, or body are fulfilled. Suppliers also use conformity assessment procedures to demonstrate to their customers that their products or related processes or systems meet particular specifications.[26]

Yet, the costs and delays attributable to unnecessary, duplicative, and unclear conformity assessment requirements are frequently cited as a key concern for U.S. exporters.[27] Indeed, many specific trade concerns raised by the United States in the TBT Committee with respect to other WTO Members' measures center on difficulties associated with the Member's conformity assessment requirements. Governments can reduce or minimize such difficulties by taking into account the risks associated with a product's failure to conform to an underlying standard or requirement when choosing the type of conformity assessment procedure to apply with respect to that standard or requirement. Governments can also reduce or minimize costs associated with conformity assessment by adopting approaches that facilitate the acceptance of the results of those procedures (*e.g.*, approaches that allow products to be tested or certified in the country of export). The TBT Committee's list of approaches that facilitate this acceptance is contained in G/TBT/1/Rev.9.

In the United States, the NTTAA directs NIST to coordinate the conformity assessment activities of Federal, state, and local entities with private sector technical standards activities and conformity assessment activities. The goal is to eliminate any unnecessary duplication of these activities. Pursuant to this statutory directive, NIST issued a *Federal Register* notice in 2000 providing guidance to Federal agencies on conformity assessment. It calls for Federal agencies to provide sound rationales, seek public comments, look to the results of other government and private sector organizations, and use international guides and standards when incorporating conformity assessment procedures in their regulations and procurement processes. Today, the

---

[25] Conformity assessment procedures take a variety of forms, including, for example, testing, certification, registration, inspection, accreditation, and verification. The entities that conduct these procedures are referred to as conformity assessment bodies and include such bodies as testing laboratories, certification bodies, and accreditation bodies. Testing laboratories, for example, test products to evaluate their performance or product characteristics while certification bodies certify that products conform to specific standards or requirements. Accreditation bodies, for example, evaluate the competency of testing and certification bodies and verify that they comply with specific standards or requirements.

[26] For an introduction to conformity assessment, see Breitenberg, Maureen, *The ABC's of the U.S. Conformity Assessment System*, NIST, 1997.

[27] See Johnson, Christopher, *Technical Barriers to Trade: Reducing the Impact of Conformity Assessment Measures*, U.S. International Trade Commission Working Paper, 2008.

conformity assessment standards and guides published by ISO and IEC are known as the "CASCO toolbox."[28]

In addition to NIST's efforts to inform and guide Federal agencies in adopting and applying conformity assessment procedures, federal agencies and private sector organizations can look to guidance in ANSI's *National Conformity Assessment Principles for the United States*. ANSI's principles provide supplemental information designed to promote increased acceptance of U.S. products in international markets through the use of competently conducted conformity assessment procedures. The TBT Agreement, NIST's guidance, and ANSI's principles all emphasize the importance of participation and use of international systems of conformity assessment in facilitating international trade.

Participation and use of international systems of conformity assessment strengthens these international systems and produces global benefits. For example, international systems for accreditation play a vital role in allowing products to be tested and certified at sites that are convenient to production facilities and reducing duplicative testing and certification requirements. International systems for accreditation enable this by establishing procedures and criteria that accreditation bodies participating in the system agree to apply when accrediting testing, certification, or other conformity assessment bodies. Accreditations issued by such entities can, in appropriate circumstances, provide governments, as well as suppliers, assurances that a body – regardless of its location – is competent to test and certify products for relevant markets.

Examples of international accreditation systems include the International Laboratory Accreditation Cooperation (ILAC) and the International Accreditation Forum (IAF). ILAC and IAF have established voluntary mutual recognition arrangements (MRAs). Under these MRAs, accreditation bodies agree to adhere to international standards and other procedures and criteria when accrediting testing and certification bodies and subject themselves to a system of peer-to-peer review to ensure that they continue to meet MRA requirements. In the United States, accreditation bodies that participate in these mutual recognition arrangements are predominately private sector entities. Increasingly, federal agencies, such as the Consumer Product Safety Commission and the Nuclear Regulatory Commission, are using international systems such as ILAC in support of their conformity assessment requirements.

---

[28] ISO/CASCO is the standards development and policy committee on conformity assessment of ISO.

VIII. U.S. Processes for Identifying Standards-Related Trade Barriers and Determining How to Address Them

The United States also maintains rigorous, interagency processes and mechanisms for identifying, reviewing, analyzing, and addressing foreign government standards-related measures that act, or may act, as barriers to U.S. trade. USTR coordinates these processes and mechanisms through the TPSC and, more specifically, its specialized TBT subgroup, the TPSC Subcommittee on Technical Barriers to Trade (TPSC Subcommittee).

The TPSC Subcommittee, comprising representatives from federal regulatory agencies and other agencies with an interest in foreign standards-related measures, meets formally at least three times a year, but maintains an ongoing process of informal consultation and coordination on all standards-related issues as they arise. Representatives of the Subcommittee include officials from the Departments of State, Agriculture, and Commerce – as well as officials from OMB and federal regulatory agencies, such as the Food and Drug Administration and the Environmental Protection Agency. The Departments of Commerce and Agriculture serve as the primary conduits for communicating information between U.S. industry and agriculture export interests, respectively, and the TPSC Subcommittee.

Information for the TPSC Subcommittee on foreign standards-related measures is collected and evaluated on a day to day basis through a variety of government channels including: the TBT Inquiry Point at NIST, the Trade Compliance Center (TCC), the Office of Standards Liaison, and the U.S. Commercial Service (UCS) in the Department of Commerce; the Foreign Agricultural Service (FAS) and its Office of Scientific and Technical Affairs (OSTA) in the Department of Agriculture; the State Department's economic officers in U.S embassies abroad; and USTR. U.S. government outreach and consultations with U.S. stakeholders generates much of the information supplied through these channels, which are further described below.

To disseminate information to U.S. stakeholders on proposed foreign notifications, NIST operates a web-based service, *Notify U.S.*, which automatically notifies registered stakeholders of measures proposed and adopted by other WTO Members in sectors of interest. These notifications alert U.S. firms and other interested stakeholders of their opportunity to comment on proposed foreign measures that may have an impact on their exports. U.S. stakeholders may provide their comments directly to the WTO Member concerned, if its domestic processes provide for that, or through NIST, which works with relevant Federal agencies to review, compile and submit comments to the WTO Member. By providing comments through NIST, U.S. stakeholders alert federal agencies to their concerns and can enable advocacy by Federal agencies on their behalf.

In 2010, NIST's U.S. WTO TBT Inquiry Point and Notification Authority processed and distributed over 45,000 information requests, including over 2,500 requests for information on standards and over 43,000 requests related to technical barriers to trade. The office distributed 112 U.S. government and industry comments to other WTO Members, and circulated 43 WTO Member comments on U.S. measures, as well as 35 WTO Member replies to U.S. comments, to relevant federal agencies. U.S. stakeholders monitor notifications of new or revised measures of other WTO Members in sectors of interest through the *Notify U.S.* early alert program, and contact U.S. officials through the government channels listed above to obtain further information, to contribute to the submission of U.S. comments, and to coordinate follow-up actions. NIST's Inquiry Point and Notification Authority hosted or participated in training for six U.S. and foreign visiting delegations interested in learning how a WTO inquiry point operates.

The TCC administers the Department of Commerce's Trade Agreements Compliance Program and coordinates efforts and resources within the Department to systematically monitor, investigate, and help ensure foreign governments' compliance with trade agreements to which the United States is a party. The TCC offers an online trade complaint hotline at *www.trade.gov/tcc* where exporters can report and obtain assistance in overcoming foreign trade barriers. The TCC helps assemble teams of specialists to investigate market access problems, including ones involving standards-related measures, as well as develop strategies to address them. Compliance teams work with affected companies or industries to establish objectives and to craft and implement compliance action plans to achieve market access.

In addition, TCC regularly provides input to the TPSC based on the information on the specific trade concerns that it collects and analyzes through this process. This information informs the TPSC's development of the appropriate U.S. position in the various multilateral and bilateral forums for addressing standards-related measures. Compliance Officers also provide on-the-ground assistance at U.S. embassies in China, India, El Salvador, Japan, and at the U.S. Mission to the European Union in Brussels. Free, online tools include the texts of more than 270 non-agricultural trade agreements plus a checklist of the kinds of trade barriers that the Program can help exporters overcome.

OSTA provides a conduit for queries and comments on foreign standards-related measures in the agricultural sector. OSTA monitors developments in relevant export markets, provides information on foreign standards-related measures through a range of publications, disseminates WTO TBT notifications from foreign governments to interested parties, and provides translation services on key export market requirements. OSTA works cooperatively with U.S. industry, as well as with technical specialists in its overseas offices and federal regulatory agencies, to develop comments and positions on specific foreign standards-related measures. In addition, FAS works through relevant international organizations to resolve agriculture-related issues arising from foreign standards-related measures.

In addition to these government channels, the TPSC Subcommittee receives information from the Industry and Agriculture Trade Advisory Committees (ITAC and ATAC, respectively). The ITAC and the ATAC help identify trade barriers and provide assessments regarding the practical realities that producers face in complying with technical regulations and conformity assessment procedures. USTR and Commerce officials meet at least quarterly with the ITAC on Standards and Technical Trade Barriers (ITAC 16), which is composed of cleared advisors from manufacturers, trade associations, standards developers, and conformity assessment bodies.[29] USTR also meets with other ITACs and advisory committees to receive advice on TBT issues affecting specific industry sectors, such as steel, chemicals, automobiles, processed foods, and textiles, or specific regulatory areas, such as labor and the environment.

---

[29] See http://www.ustr.gov/Who_We_Are/List_of_USTR_Advisory_Committees.html.

In developing the U.S. position on any foreign standards-related measure, the TPSC Subcommittee takes into account how the United States regulates the same or similar products. Regulatory agency officials on the TBT TPSC Subcommittee also provide important information on the technical and scientific aspects of particular foreign standards-related measures, as well as insights on cooperative efforts through international organizations that may be relevant to the issue. The TPSC Subcommittee factors the views that regulatory agencies express into the positions that the United States takes in multilateral, regional, and bilateral trade discussions regarding standards-related measures. Particularly in the area of emerging technologies where standards-related activities are nascent, the technical, scientific, and policy advice that regulatory agencies provide is critical in formulating U.S. views.

IX. U.S. Engagement on Standards-Related Measures in International, Regional, and Bilateral Fora

Overview of U.S. Engagement on Standards-Related Measures

The United States maintains a broad and active agenda of engagement with foreign governments to prevent unnecessary obstacles to trade and to resolve specific trade concerns arising from standards-related measures. As noted above, the TBT Committee is the principal multilateral forum for engagement on trade issues relating to standards-related measures. The mechanisms for cooperation on these measures in U.S. FTAs also play a vital role in facilitating U.S. efforts to prevent and resolve trade concerns. In addition, U.S. agencies seek to prevent potential technical barriers from emerging by engaging in multilateral, regional, and bilateral cooperative activities, information exchanges, technical assistance, and negotiations on specific agreements. These efforts are aimed at helping other governments design effective and well-conceived standards-related measures, with the goal of producing better regulatory outcomes and facilitating trade.

U.S. government cooperative efforts and information exchanges with developing countries can assist firms in those countries build their capacity to comply with foreign standards-related measures. As developing country producers increase their participation in global supply chains, they need a better understanding of foreign technical requirements and strategies to consistently meet those requirements. Cooperative activities can also serve to prevent localized high-profile incidents of the type that can disrupt trade across all markets and damage both producer reputations and consumer confidence. Close coordination among trade, regulatory, and standards officials with highly specialized technical expertise is required in order to carry out cooperation and information exchange initiatives that successfully meet these objectives. The United States provides bilateral technical assistance and capacity building to developing countries on standards-related activities through the U.S. Agency for International Development (USAID), the U.S. Trade and Development Agency (USTDA), and the Commerce Department's Commercial Law Development Program (CLDP), Market Development Cooperator Program (NDCP), and NIST. USDA's FAS also provides technical assistance on standards related to food trade. These agencies have broader missions and generally provide standards-related capacity building assistance as a component of a specific project or mission.

To reduce the negative impact on trade from divergences in technical requirements across markets, the United States negotiates bilateral, regional, and multilateral MRAs with U.S. trading partners. These agreements establish procedures for each party to accept the results of conformity assessment procedures for specified products carried out in the other party's territory or to accept the other government's technical specifications for those products as sufficient to meet its own requirements. MRAs with trading partners that have a regulatory approach compatible with that of the United States and a similar level of technical capacity can help facilitate trade in select sectors where trade flows are significant and technical requirements can be complex, such as in the telecommunication equipment sector.

NIST maintains a complete inventory of the government-to-government MRAs to which the United States is a party. It also maintains a listing of the accreditation requirements for conformity assessment bodies under each of these MRAs and a list of conformity assessment bodies that NIST has designated pursuant to each MRA as competent to perform tests or certify products to ensure they conform to the other MRA party's technical requirements. (The Federal Communications Commission (FCC) website provides useful background information on U.S. MRAs in the telecommunications sector and examples of how they work.)

The United States also seeks to reduce foreign technical barriers by concluding "equivalency" arrangements with other governments. One recent example is the June 2009 exchange of equivalency determinations between USDA and Canada's Food Inspection Agency on organic agricultural products. As a result of that exchange, U.S. producers that a USDA-accredited agent certifies as meeting U.S. National Organic Program standards do not need to be certified under the Canada's National Organic Standard in order to market their products in Canada as "organic." The exchange provides for Canadian producers to receive a similar accommodation for products they export to the United States.

U.S. engagement on standards-related measures in various international and regional fora is detailed below. U.S. bilateral engagement with its trading partners on standards-related measures is detailed in individual Country Specific Reports in Section X.

TBT Committee

Specific Trade Concerns

The U.S. government actively seeks to prevent and eliminate technical barriers to trade through the TBT Committee, with its focused WTO Member-driven agenda. The Committee dedicates a significant portion of each of its three annual meetings to affording Members the opportunity to raise specific trade concerns on measures that other Members have proposed or adopted. WTO Members may also use Committee sessions to share experiences, case studies, or concerns relating to cross-cutting issues regarding how Members are implementing the TBT Agreement. The TBT Committee often holds workshops or other events on special topics alongside its formal meetings. On the margins of each meeting, Members engage in informal bilateral and plurilateral meetings to clarify and resolve specific trade concerns and to discuss how to resolve other issues of mutual interest.

In 2010, the United States raised specific trade concerns regarding 20 to 30 foreign TBT measures at each TBT Committee meeting and in the informal meetings it held with individual or groups of WTO Members. The details and status of many of the specific trade concerns that the United States raised in, and on the margins of, the TBT Committee sessions are described in Section X of this report. As elaborated in Section X, U.S. interventions in the TBT Committee, and on its margins, have helped resolve a number of standards-related concerns affecting U.S. trade.

The Committee's annual review of its activities is contained in G/TBT/29, which includes a thumbnail description of the specific trade concerns that WTO Members raised, as well as identifies the Members that raised them.

Triennial Reviews of the TBT Agreement

The TBT Agreement calls for the TBT Committee to review the implementation and operation of the Agreement every three years. These triennial reviews provide an important opportunity for WTO Members to clarify particular provisions of the Agreement. Triennial reviews have resulted in a significant body of agreed recommendations and decisions, contained in G/TBT/1/Rev.9, which are intended to strengthen and improve the operation of the TBT Agreement.

In November 2009, the TBT Committee completed its *Fifth Triennial Review of the Operation and Implementation of the Agreement on Technical Barriers to Trade Under Article 15.4.* Numerous suggestions that the United States put forward for purposes of the review figure prominently among the Committee's recommendations, including regulatory cooperation, good regulatory practice, internal coordination, transparency, and international standards. These recommendations are set out in G/TBT/26. The Committee also established an important and ambitious work program on conformity assessment in the report on the review. The report and its recommendations establish the focus of the TBT Committee's work program.

Regulatory cooperation featured prominently in the discussions under the review. The United States advocated for greater regulatory cooperation in a joint submission with its NAFTA partners (G/TBT/W/317). Regulatory cooperation is an avenue for reducing unnecessary technical divergences as well as for achieving better regulatory outcomes – both of which can help to facilitate and expand trade. For example, regulatory efforts that effectively reduce the incidence of unsafe products benefit both the consumers who purchase those products as well as the producers that produce those products. The TBT Committee supported the proposal from the NAFTA countries, and agreed to hold a workshop to explore the variety of approaches to regulatory cooperation. The workshop is tentatively scheduled for November 2011. The Committee will be looking to use the workshop to identify avenues to promote greater regulatory alignment.

During the review, a U.S. submission on how to identify the need to regulate, G/TBT/W/285, also factored into the TBT Committee's discussions and recommendations as an important component of GRP discussions. Other Members showed significant interest in advancing work on GRP, with Brazil, Canada, China, Costa Rica, Jordan, Korea, Israel, and New Zealand submitting papers and comments relating to GRP issues. GRP carries the potential to help WTO Members in the following ways: enhance their capacity for market surveillance; apply risk analysis in developing regulation; produce clarity in the definition of regulatory objectives; facilitate communication with industry, consumers and other stakeholders; provide a basis for effective training; maximize the benefits of trade facilitation; and generally ensure policy integrity. Going forward, the TBT Committee will compile guidelines and discuss mechanisms for Members to implement GRP.

In the course of the review, the United States also spearheaded in-depth discussions on the benefits and challenges of greater use of international standards. Worldwide use of international standards facilitates trade by helping firms achieve economies of scale in production, source low-cost global inputs, and achieve greater acceptance for their products across countries. In March 2009, the Committee held a workshop on overcoming challenges and instituting best practices relating to the development and use of international standards to help firms in developing countries participate more fully in global markets. Experts from Peru, Pakistan, Brazil, Colombia, Chile, Egypt, and Kenya presented practical case studies illustrating how the use of international standards yielded positive economic benefits to their economies. Several developing country Members stressed the challenges confronting their producers in complying with multiple or conflicting standards around the world. Many U.S. exporters strongly support the principle that governments should avoid mandating unnecessary local specifications for globally traded products.

Members also reaffirmed the importance during the review of both the TBT Agreement's *Code of Good Practice* for developing, adopting, and using standards and the *2000 Committee Decision* on the development of international standards. The *Code* calls on Members to ensure that their standardizing bodies at the central level of government do not adopt standards that create unnecessary obstacles to trade, and to take reasonable measures to ensure that standardizing bodies at sub-central levels of government as well as private standardizing bodies do not produce standards that create unnecessary obstacles to trade. The *2000 Committee Decision* states that processes for developing international standards should be transparent, consensus-based, and open to all interested parties. Both the *Code* and the *2000 Committee Decision* seek to avoid duplication in standards development. At the conclusion of the review, the TBT Committee agreed to share experiences and examine more closely the ways in which Members implement both the *Code* and the *2000 Committee Decision*.

In previous triennial reviews, the Committee's work on conformity assessment focused on information exchange. In the course of those reviews, the Committee held several events addressing conformity assessment[30] and developed an indicative list of approaches that Members can use to facilitate the acceptance of results of conformity assessment procedures performed in other countries (see G/TBT/1/Rev.9). In the *Fifth Triennial Review*, Members agreed to continue to exchange information on this subject, but broadened the scope of that exchange to include the criteria, methods of analysis, and concepts that Members use to inform their evaluation and choose conformity assessment procedures for specific purposes, including in the context of a risk management framework. Further, based on these exchanges, the TBT Committee agreed to initiate work on developing practical guidelines on how to choose and design efficient and effective mechanisms aimed at strengthening the implementation of the conformity assessment provisions of the TBT Agreement.

Finally, during the review, the Committee continued its focus on how Members are carrying out those provisions of the TBT Agreement that provide for Members to give notice and comment on proposed technical regulations and conformity assessment procedures. The TBT's notice and comment rules, and the requirement for Members to take comments into account in finalizing the measures they notify, are fundamental to preventing and minimizing unnecessary obstacle to trade. Members discussed and reaffirmed the significant body of recommendations and decisions on these transparency procedures that the Committee had established in earlier reviews. In addition, reflecting the increase in standards-related regulatory activity of local governments (*e.g.*, at the state and provincial level) affecting trade, the Committee called for

---

[30] These events were: (i) a Symposium on Conformity Assessment Procedures was held on 8-9 June 1999 (G/TBT/9, 13 November 2000, Annex 1); (ii) a Special Meeting dedicated to Conformity Assessment Procedures was held on 29 June 2004 (G/TBT/M/33/Add.1, 21 October 2004); (iii) a Workshop on Supplier's Declaration of Conformity (SDoC) was held on 21 March 2005 (Annex 1 of G/TBT/M/35, 24 May 2005); and, (iv) a Workshop on the Different Approaches to Conformity Assessment, including on the Acceptance of Conformity Assessment Results, was held on 16-17 March 2006 (G/TBT/M/38/Add.1, 6 June 2006).

better coordination between central and local governments to improve Members' implementation of the TBT Agreement's transparency provisions.

In 2011, the Committee will continue its work based on the conclusions of the *Fifth Review.*

APEC

2011: The U.S. APEC Year

The APEC [31] forum is the Asia-Pacific region's premier inter-governmental economic organization. Its core mission is to strengthen regional economic integration by addressing barriers to trade and investment. APEC's 21 member economies comprise nearly half the world's population and more than half of the global economy. These member economies account for 55 percent of global GDP, purchase 58 percent of U.S. goods exports, and comprise a market of 2.7 billion customers. In fact, seven of America's top 15 trade partners are in APEC. As host of APEC in 2011, the United States has an historic opportunity to advance a trade and investment agenda that will sustain the economic recovery by supporting the growth in trade, investment and jobs in the region. The United States will chair a series of ministerial and other meetings throughout 2011, including the Trade Ministers meeting in Big Sky, Montana on May 19-20. The APEC year will culminate with a heads-of-state meeting in Honolulu, Hawaii in November hosted by President Obama.

In its role as APEC chair, the United States will continue to emphasize the importance of setting APEC policies to accelerate growth and create jobs across the region by addressing specific concerns for improving the trade and investment environment. The United States will also give priority to concrete initiatives that will build towards a "seamless regional economy" by achieving practical, concrete, and ambitious outcomes in three priority areas:

(1) strengthening regional economic integration and expanding trade;

(2) promoting green growth; and

(3) expanding regulatory cooperation and advancing regulatory convergence.

Under U.S. leadership, standards-related issues will be a key priority in 2011. For example, the United States is leading an initiative in 2011 to encourage APEC economies to avoid imposing unnecessary technical barriers related to emerging green technologies, including commercial green buildings, solar technologies, and smart grid. The United States is also working to encourage APEC economies to adopt standards and conformity assessment procedures that promote greener growth by applying ISO 50001, an international standard that will establish a framework for industrial plants, commercial facilities, or entire organizations to manage their energy use.

---

[31] The APEC members are Australia, Brunei Darussalam, Canada, Chile, China, Hong Kong China, Indonesia, Japan, Korea, Malaysia, Mexico, New Zealand, Papua New Guinea, Peru, the Philippines, Russia, Singapore, Taiwan, Thailand, Vietnam, and the United States.

Additionally, the United States will seek agreement by its APEC partners to take steps to strengthen implementation of good regulatory practices, including regulatory impact assessments, designed to prevent unnecessary barriers to trade. This initiative fits well with the work that APEC has conducted since its inception in 1989 to promote good regulatory practices, encourage greater alignment of international standards, reform testing and certification programs, and advance development of a standards and conformity assessment infrastructure in the region.

APEC Subcommittee on Standards and Conformance

In 1994, APEC established the Subcommittee on Standards and Conformance (SCSC) with the goal of better aligning the divergent approaches to standards and conformance issues that economies in the region have adopted. The SCSC works to reduce the negative impact of these divergences on trade and investment, as well as to facilitate increased market access through improved standards and conformance procedures. The SCSC seeks to improve these measures by promoting approaches that embody the APEC principles of market-driven interdependence and open regionalism. The SCSC does not develop standards and does not support the use of regional standards. Rather, the SCSC seeks to encourage APEC economies to align their standards-related measures with international standards.

The SCSC is unique among inter-governmental forums in that it regularly brings together trade policy officials, representatives of national standards bodies, and other technical specialists[32] to advance standards-related goals through cooperation. Regulatory officials often participate in SCSC special events and initiatives. The SCSC also invites private sector representatives with specific expertise to participate in its special events. The United States has established several public-private partnerships to advance priority issues in the SCSC. These partnerships provide the SCSC with invaluable access to technical expertise and resources – and provide critical information on the practical realities that producers face in complying with technical regulations, and that governments confront in developing standards and using conformity assessment procedures.

The SCSC is a valuable forum for garnering support for policy priorities, conducting capacity building activities, and building consensus among APEC economies on standards-related measures. The Committee makes use of studies, surveys, workshops, training, and other events to achieve these objectives. The SCSC work is member-driven, with officials of different APEC countries working collaboratively to develop and implement projects and initiatives. These efforts are designed to promote greater alignment to international standards, pursue recognition arrangements for conformity assessments, encourage cooperation to develop "technical infrastructure," and improve implementation of good regulatory practices, including through activities to promote greater understanding and cooperation on regulatory issues. The SCSC addresses both TBT and SPS issues.

---

[32] Representatives from the APEC "Specialized Regional Bodies" (SRBs) participate in the SCSC as technical experts. The five APEC SRBs are: the Pacific Area Standards Congress (PASC), the Asia-Pacific Metrology Program (APMP), the Pacific Accreditation Cooperation (PAC), the Asia Pacific Legal Metrology Forum (APLMF) and the Asia-Pacific Laboratory Accreditation Cooperation (APLAC). For a summary of work of the SRBs, see "The Role of the APEC Specialist Regional Bodies: Elements of the Standards and Conformance Infrastructure" March 2008.

Over the years, the SCSC has made important contributions to advancing progress and understanding on the trade aspects of standards-related matters, both in the region and internationally. In its work on conformity assessments, the SCSC has published reports and surveys on topics such as suppliers' declaration of conformity, market surveillance, and the effectiveness of MRAs. The SCSC established a "Voluntary Alignment Program" that has identified priority areas for member economies to align their measures with international standards and monitored the progress that each economy has made in adopting international standards. The SCSC has also adopted a strategic plan for improving technical infrastructure that identifies capacity building priorities for each developing APEC economy in the areas of standards, accreditation, laboratory accreditation, metrology, and legal metrology.

The United States is leading a number of initiatives in the SCSC, including public-private partnerships, such as the APEC Toy Safety Initiative and the Partnership Training Institute Network (PTIN) of the Food Safety Cooperation Forum (FSCF), both of which are described in greater detail below. The United States is continuing its leadership by hosting the SCSC's 6th Conference on Good Regulatory Practice, March 1-2, 2011, and by co-chairing the SCSC's Trade Facilitation Task Force (TFTF), which brings trade and technical experts together on a regular basis to share information and cooperate on product-related environmental standards-related measures.

The APEC Toy Safety Initiative

Following high-profile incidents involving recalls of unsafe toys in 2007, APEC Leaders directed their officials to work to strengthen product safety standards and practices in the region without creating unnecessary obstacles to trade. The SCSC responded in 2008 by launching the U.S.-led APEC Toy Safety Initiative. Co-sponsored by the U.S. Toy Industry Association, the goals of the APEC Toy Safety Initiative are to strengthen toy safety, increase transparency, promote better regulatory alignment, and reduce unnecessary obstacles to trade that may arise as a result of toy safety systems. The Initiative sought to advance these goals through the "*Regulator Dialogue on Toy Safety*," held in Singapore in August 2009, and the *Survey of Toy Safety Regulators* delivered at the "*Open Dialogue on Toy Safety for All Stakeholders*," held in conjunction with the Hong Kong Toy Fair in January 2010.[33]

In 2011, toy safety regulators from the APEC region met under the auspices of the International Consumer Product Safety and Health Organization to review progress on the goals they set in 2009 seeking to increase alignment of toy safety reference standards in the region. This work will continue.

Partnership Training Institute Network of the Food Safety Cooperation Forum

Concerns about food safety in the Asia-Pacific region have risen sharply in recent years and have spurred a collective mandate from leaders of the APEC countries to improve food safety standards and practices in the region without creating unnecessary impediments to trade. In response, the SCSC established the FSCF in 2007 with the goal of improving food safety

---

[33] All of the agendas, presentations and reports on the APEC Toy Safety Initiative's activities are available on the website of the Toy Industry Association: http://www.toyassociation.org.

regulatory systems in APEC economies, including food inspection, assurance, and certification systems that are consistent with WTO Members' rights and obligations under both the SPS and TBT Agreements.[34]

The FSCF seeks to increase food safety and facilitate trade in safe food by addressing capacity building opportunities for APEC member economies in priority areas such as information sharing, food safety regulatory systems, and food inspection. In 2008, APEC leaders called for increased capacity building to improve technical competence and understanding of food safety management among stakeholders in the food supply chain, which include regulators, growers, packers, handlers, storage providers, processors, manufacturers, retailers, and food service providers.

In 2008, the United States, in collaboration with stakeholders from the private sector and academia, spearheaded the establishment of the Partnership Training Institute Network (FSCF PTIN). FSCF PTIN combines the expertise and resources of industry, government, and academia to strengthen and augment the FSCF's efforts in addressing capacity building needs in the region. The goal of the FSCF PTIN is to facilitate trade and protect public health by building the capacity of stakeholders in the food supply chain to use international standards and best practices in food safety management from production to consumption, and by creating a network of institutes and experts to conduct training of food safety regulators in international best practices in food safety. In 2010, the FSCF PTIN conducted training workshops on the following subjects:

- **Export Certificates.** While the use of export certificates can facilitate trade in food and agricultural products, the procedures for export certification have grown increasingly more complex and varied as regulators around the region strive to assure food safety throughout the supply chain. The training provided by FSCF PTIN to food safety regulators on this subject provided guidance on how to avoid imposing unnecessary certification requirements, how to create generic certificates, and how to promote the use of electronic certification in the region.

- **Food Recall Systems**. Training provided by FSCF PTIN on this subject focused on helping government officials develop recall protocols for different food industry sectors, as well as streamline their recall systems based on experiences in economies with stable and effective recall systems. The goal of this work was to better prepare APEC member economies to deal with outbreaks and to implement effective and efficient food recalls.

- **Food Safety Curricula**. The FSCF PTIN hosted a workshop on best practices in the development and delivery of food safety curricula, bringing together a core group of food safety experts from the APEC economies to address ways to develop and deliver enduring food safety training in the region. The group developed a strategy and roadmap for reviewing existing publicly available materials, identifying gaps in coverage, and using this information to adopt and build a generic set of training materials that can be used to meet food safety training priorities identified by APEC member economies.

---

[34] The FSCF covers both SPS and TBT issues. For convenience, the activities of the FSCF are included in the *2010 TBT Report* rather than *2010 SPS Report*.

- **Supply Chains**. The FSCF PTIN also sponsored a three-day training aimed at helping food regulators in APEC economies understand and apply best practices and use innovative technologies in developing food safety plans for supply chains. The goal was to ensure that suppliers provide products that meet applicable regulatory, legal, and contractual food safety standards in the relevant APEC economy.

Trade Facilitation Task Force (TFTF)

The proliferation and diversity of product-related environmental regulations, particularly those of the European Union, prompted the need for an APEC forum to promote information exchange and cooperation to reduce the potentially adverse trade impact on APEC economies from these emerging technical requirements. In 2006, the SCSC established the Trade Facilitation Task Force (TFTF). The TFTF, co-chaired by Korea and the United States, brings together trade and technical experts to exchange information on specific trade concerns affecting APEC economies (whether imposed by other APEC economies or countries outside the APEC region) and to promote cooperation in international standardization activities associated with product-specific environmental regulations. Experts from industry, academia, international or regional bodies, and other relevant authorities participate in TFTF activities.

In September 2010 the TFTF met in Sendai, Japan to exchange information and promote cooperation on the trade and technical aspects of current work related to carbon emission estimation and sustainability.

Trans-Pacific Partnership (TPP)

The Trans-Pacific Partnership (TPP) is a key initiative through which the United States seeks to advance the multi-faceted U.S. trade and investment interests in the Asia-Pacific region by negotiating an ambitious, 21st-century regional trade agreement along with Australia, Brunei Darussalam, Chile, Malaysia, New Zealand, Peru, Singapore, and Vietnam. The TPP has begun with this initial group of like-minded countries with the goal of creating a platform for regional integration across the region.

In the TPP negotiations addressing standards-related issues, the United States is emphasizing several key themes, including regulatory transparency, encouraging the use of good regulatory practices, and providing for TPP governments to accept the results of conformity assessment procedures carried out in TPP partner countries. The overall U.S. objective is to establish rules and disciplines for standards-related measures that reduce the likelihood that TPP countries will create or maintain unnecessary technical barriers to trade.

In the U.S. view, open and transparent procedures for developing technical regulations, standards, and conformity assessment procedures are key to avoiding unnecessary technical barriers to trade. In particular, where regulators provide early notice to interested parties at home and abroad that they are considering adopting new measures, the interested parties can help regulators obtain the information they need to design the measures in a way that avoids placing unnecessary burdens on local and foreign producers. Moreover, when regulators use transparent procedures in developing regulations, they also help ensure that both domestic and foreign stakeholders will view the final regulations as legitimate. In addition, transparent implementation of measures and reasonable compliance periods will enhance legal certainty and predictability for suppliers and make it easier for them to comply.

Transparent procedures in developing regulations are also vital in crafting high quality, science-based regulations. In particular, these procedures help governments avoid adopting unneeded, inappropriate, or overly burdensome technical regulations, while enhancing the competitiveness.

The United States is also working to reach agreement in the TPP negotiations on the principle that suppliers do not need to have their facilities inspected more than once or have their products tested more than once in order to demonstrate that they comply with technical regulations and standards in place in a particular export market. In addition, the United States is seeking commitment from each TPP government that it will permit suppliers in other TPP countries to allow testing to be carried out by a conformity assessment body of their choice, regardless of where it is located, as long as the body meets the importing country's criteria for approved assessment bodies.

Regulatory Cooperation Fora

The United States participates in three bilateral regulatory cooperation forums aimed at promoting regulatory best practices and aligning regulatory approaches in economically significant sectors.

European Union

Last year's report provided a comprehensive summary of the EU's approach to standards-related measures and its trade-restrictive effects on U.S. exports to the EU (see pages 45-50 of the *2010 TBT Report*). The EU's approach, and its efforts to encourage governments around the world to adopt its approach, continues to present one of the biggest strategic challenges for the United States in the area of standards-related measures. In 2010, U.S. officials worked to develop a more comprehensive strategy for addressing this challenge in existing bilateral fora, such as the Transatlantic Economic Council (TEC) and the United States – European Union High-Level Regulatory Cooperation Forum (HLRCF), to encourage systemic changes in the EU approach.

The TEC is designed to give high-level political direction to bilateral initiatives aimed at promoting increased bilateral trade, job creation, and economic growth through deeper transatlantic economic integration. The HLRCF, comprising U.S. and EU regulatory and policy officials, oversees a program of bilateral cooperation on horizontal and sectoral regulatory issues. The group has convened in each of the past three TEC meetings to identify projects for the TEC to consider. During its December 2010 meeting, the TEC called for the HLRCF to undertake several cross-cutting (or "horizontal) cooperation initiatives, among them: (1) developing a shared set of principles and best practices for regulation; (2) exploring mechanisms for identifying candidate sectors for upstream regulatory cooperation; and (3) crafting a package of joint improvements to each side's approach to the use of standards in regulation.

Efforts to Develop a Shared Set of Principles and Best Practices

Pursuant to the TEC's instructions, the United States and the European Commission agreed to five regulatory principles to reinforce and improve bilateral regulatory cooperation to ensure that regulations in the United States and the EU protect public health, welfare, safety and the environment while also promoting trade, economic growth, and job creation. These principles include the following:

- Transparency and openness, allowing participation by stakeholders and the public;

- Consideration of costs and benefits;

- Careful analysis of alternatives;

- Selection of the least burdensome approach; and

- Use of flexible tools, promoting freedom of choice and free markets.

On the basis of these shared principles, the United States and the European Commission further agreed to the following best regulatory practices:

- Regulations should be adopted through a transparent and open process that, to the extent feasible, promotes accountability and participation, with adequate time, opportunity, and accessible tools (including the Internet) for public comment in advance;

- Regulations should be adopted only after a careful assessment of the costs and benefits (both quantitative and qualitative) of regulatory proposals and should be based on the best available science and a reasoned determination that the benefits of the chosen approach justify the costs;

- Regulations should be adopted only after careful consideration of reasonable alternatives, both more stringent and less stringent, including non-regulatory options;

- Regulations should be tailored to impose the least burden on society, consistent with achieving regulatory objectives, and to minimize adverse impacts on competition, job growth, innovation, entrepreneurship, and international trade and investment;

- Regulations should not impose unnecessarily divergent, burdensome, or duplicative requirements between the United States and the EU;

- To the extent feasible, regulations should promote flexibility and freedom of choice, through, for example, disclosure requirements and performance standards rather than design standards; and

- Existing regulations should be reevaluated periodically and, to the extent feasible and appropriate, modified, expanded, streamlined, or repealed in light of experience.

On the basis of the agreement on principles and best practices, the United States has urged the EU to agree to establish new bilateral mechanisms to promote early warning of planned regulatory actions and consultation with outside parties, including:

- Use of on-line planning tools and documents to improve transparency and understanding of the regulatory lifecycle, and to highlight actions available for public comment;

41

- Soliciting input from international stakeholders on regulatory actions under review to help prevent unnecessary divergence, burdens, and duplicative regulatory requirements, including (when feasible and appropriate) meetings with senior-level officials and international stakeholders; and

- Ensuring that proposals to supplement or modify existing regulations are made available for public comment, and procedures for public comment are open and accessible, with comment periods generally lasting at least 60 days.

The United States has also urged the EU to create new bilateral mechanisms to promote regulatory cooperation and collaboration, including by:

- Exploring new ways to use planning tools and documents to enable more opportunities for cooperation and collaboration with foreign governments and external stakeholders, and to encourage more advice and more useful comments;

- Expanding the use of on-line planning tools and documents to exchange regulatory information and display materials throughout the regulatory lifecycle in real time and in an intuitive, graphic manner;

- Including senior officials from the OMB and the European Commission in meetings on regulatory issues; and

- Issuing annual notices to the public to solicit recommendations on potential sectors to consider for inclusion in initiatives to promote bilateral regulatory convergence or for other types of cooperative activities that the HLRCF should explore.

The United States has also urged the EU to consider establishing bilateral mechanisms for enhancing regulatory transparency, including procedures to broaden participation by stakeholders and the public in the development of U.S. and EU regulatory measures.

Regulating Nanotechnology

The United States and EU identified nanotechnology as one initial area in which regulatory cooperation might be possible. U.S. officials briefed the EU on the U.S. government's accelerated and robust efforts to develop a consensus approach to nanotechnology. Among other things, U.S. officials discussed with their EU counterparts a common definition of "nanomaterial" and the two sides agreed to take a risk-based approach to regulating nanotechnology, which they agreed was more appropriate than considering hazards alone. The two sides also agreed to base their analyses on the best available science on nanotechnology, and to continue to cooperate, including sharing best practices and research.

Voluntary Standards

During the December 2010 discussion, the United States and EU agreed to "build bridges" between their respective approaches on the use of voluntary standards in regulation, despite maintaining very different overall approaches to standards development and use. In a December 16, 2010 joint statement, the HLRCF identified as primary areas of focus efforts to enhance transparency and meaningful stakeholder participation in each side's processes for developing standards and regulations, and called for the two sides to develop by the next HLRCF meeting a set of proposals to implement these principles.

The United States will continue to press these issues with the EU during the remainder of 2011.

Mexico

In May 2010, President Obama and Mexican President Calderón committed to enhance significantly the economic competitiveness and the economic well-being of the United States and Mexico through improved regulatory cooperation. The Presidents directed the creation of a United States – Mexico High-Level Regulatory Cooperation Council (HLRCC), comprising senior-level regulatory, trade, and foreign affairs officials from each country.

The HLRCC will seek to promote several goals, including:

- Making regulations in the two countries simpler and more compatible, increasing simplification, and reducing compliance burdens without compromising health, public safety, environmental protection, or national security;

- Increasing regulatory transparency to build national regulatory frameworks designed to achieve higher levels of competitiveness and promote development;

- Simplifying regulatory requirements through public involvement;

- Improving and simplifying regulation by strengthening their analytic base; and

- Increasing bilateral technical cooperation.

The HLRCC held its inaugural meeting in Washington, DC on September 13, 2010. Participants discussed their shared commitment to regulatory cooperation on key issues. The two sides began considering sectors with high levels of integration that might be subject to HLRCC focus. Participants also discussed systemic issues, such as transparency mechanisms and analytical techniques, how the two governments use standards as regulatory tools, and steps the two sides could take to provide each other with an "early warning" of significant anticipated regulatory.

In March 2011, the U.S. Department of Commerce's International Trade Administration (ITA) published a *Federal Register* notice requesting views from the public on cooperative activities that the United States should pursue with Mexico under the HLRCC or Canada under the parallel Council that the United States and Canada have established (discussed below). U.S. officials will consider these suggestions together with the recommendations Canada and Mexico elicit in their own public outreach efforts with a view to identifying areas of unnecessary regulatory divergences in North American that may be disrupting U.S. exports and addressing them in the appropriate Council.

Canada

In February 2011, President Obama and Canadian Prime Minister Harper directed the creation of a United States – Canada Regulatory Cooperation Council (RCC), composed of senior regulatory, trade, and foreign affairs officials from each government. The RCC has a two-year mandate to promote economic growth, job creation, and benefits to U.S. and Canadian consumers and businesses by enhancing regulatory transparency and coordination.

The United States and Canada will work through the RCC to provide early notice of regulations with potential cross-border effects, strengthen the analytical basis of their regulations, and help make their regulations more compatible. The RCC will focus its work on sectors characterized by high levels of integration, significant growth potential, and rapidly evolving technologies.

Doha Round Negotiations Regarding Standards-Related Measures

The United States has tabled three proposals in the WTO's Doha Round of Trade Negotiations on Non-Agricultural Market Access (NAMA) aimed at reducing standards-related non-tariff barriers (NTBs). These proposals cover: (1) textiles, apparel, footwear, and travel goods (TAFT);[35] (2) electronic goods;[36] and (3) automotive goods.[37] WTO Member "senior officials" have set all three of these proposals for priority negotiations as part of the overall NAMA NTB negotiations and the proposals were included in the NAMA Chair's December 2008 negotiating text.[38]

Each of the three proposals seeks to facilitate trade in specific sectors for which U.S. industry has expressed particular concern about standards-related NTBs. For example, the TAFT proposal grew out of U.S. industry concerns that the differing approaches that WTO Members take to labeling requirements and sudden changes in those requirements can impose substantial costs and burdens on producers while also increasing the time it takes to bring these products to the market. In many cases, these costs are then passed on to importers and consumers. The three U.S. proposals aim to address sector-specific issues of this nature by building on existing TBT Agreement disciplines. In addition, the three U.S. proposals also create new and enhanced disciplines in areas such as transparency, good regulatory practice, international standards, and conformity assessment procedures, while at the same time ensuring that regulators retain the ability to meet legitimate policy objectives.

During the last year, all three U.S. proposals were discussed in detail among WTO Members, with the most significant progress being made on the U.S. textiles proposal and on transparency provisions common to all three proposals. The chair of the negotiations created small groups to

---

[35] Understanding on the Interpretation of the Agreement on Technical Barriers to Trade with respect to the Labelling of Textiles, Clothing, Footwear, and Travel Goods (TN/MA/W/93/Rev.2, 8 November 2010).

[36] Understanding on Non-Tariff Barriers Pertaining to the Electrical Safety and Electromagnetic Compatibility (EMC) of Electronic Goods (TN/MA/W/105/Rev.3, 26 November 2010).

[37] Understanding on Non-Tariff Barriers Pertaining to Standards, Technical Regulations, and Conformity Assessment Procedures for Automotive Products (TN/MA/W/120, 9 July 2010).

[38] Fourth Revision of the Draft Modalities for Non-Agricultural Market Access (TN/MA/W/103/Rev.3, 6 December 2008. The list of proposals is in paragraph 24.

facilitate greater discussions on these initiatives among the WTO Members with the most substantial interest in the respective subject matter. The United States is participating vigorously in these small groups with the hope of achieving consensus while also continuing to advocate for its autos and electronics proposals.

Textiles

The TAFT proposal, which the United States introduced along with the EU, Mauritius, Sri Lanka, and Ukraine, seeks to facilitate trade in textiles, apparel, footwear, and travel goods through provisions that would promote greater alignment of labeling requirements. In this manner, the U.S. textiles proposal would reduce costs for suppliers, exporters, and consumers. The proposal would promote greater alignment of labeling requirements by encouraging Members to limit their labeling requirements to certain subjects (such as care instructions or fiber content) while at the same time discouraging Members from imposing other requirements (such as requirements for labels to be certified or made of certain materials). The U.S. proposal would also encourage Members to use non-permanent labels instead of permanent labels where appropriate. Finally, the U.S. TAFT proposal calls for strong transparency rules, which are discussed in greater detail in the section below.

Transparency

All three U.S. proposals (autos, electronics, and textiles) set out rules to enhance regulatory transparency and promote good regulatory practices. These rules seek to ensure that U.S. industry and other relevant stakeholders are able to participate on a non-discriminatory basis in the process by which other WTO Members develop standards-related measures by guaranteeing that stakeholders could submit comments on proposed regulatory measures, have the relevant WTO Members take their comments into account, and see a response to their comments no later than the date the Member publishes the final measure. These rules will help U.S. stakeholders influence the development of standards-related measures that other Members adopt and help reduce the chances that those measures will disadvantage U.S. exports.

The U.S. transparency proposals would also increase the likelihood that regulators around the world base their regulations on similar data and reach similar conclusions regarding the risks associated with a particular product and the appropriate measures to mitigate those risks. In addition, the U.S. proposals encourage regulators to develop and adopt better informed and effective regulatory measures. For these reasons, the rules set out in the proposal will help U.S. producers increase their exports to different markets around the world.

To achieve these transparency-related goals, the U.S. proposals on autos, electronics, and textiles each include provisions that would require WTO Members to notify the TBT Committee of the technical regulations and conformity assessment procedures they propose to develop, regardless of whether these measures are based on international standards. This would build on existing TBT Agreement obligations (which require Members to notify the TBT Committee only if they measures they propose are not based on international standards), and would ensure that stakeholders can learn of proposed regulations that may affect their ability to export to a particular market. In addition, each of the U.S. proposals would provide a greater opportunity than is currently guaranteed under WTO rules for interested parties to comment on proposed regulations before they are adopted.

The U.S. transparency proposals also seek to ensure good regulatory practices in the sectors they cover. For example, the proposals require Members regularly to review their relevant technical regulations and conformity assessment procedures and ensure that they have adequate domestic procedures in place to review the actions their regulators take to apply them. In addition, the proposals would require Members that are preparing or proposing to adopt a technical regulation or conformity assessment procedure to consider the costs of complying with the proposed measure. Further, the proposals would require Members to consider regulatory and non-regulatory alternatives before adopting a technical regulation, or conformity assessment procedure.

Autos and Electronics-Specific Provisions

The U.S. autos and electronics proposal contain a number of proposed rules similar to the standards-related provisions of U.S. FTAs. Although discussions on these proposals have not advanced as far as those for the U.S. proposals on textiles and transparency, the United States continues vigorously to advocate for them.

The U.S. auto and electronics proposals include rules that would encourage standardizing bodies around the world to develop standards that are globally and technically relevant and to ensure that the procedures these bodies follow to develop standards include a meaningful opportunity for U.S. exporters and other stakeholders to provide comments before the standards are adopted. In particular, the U.S. proposals would clarify that a standard will only be considered an international standard within the meaning of the TBT Agreement if it is developed in accordance with the six principles of the *2000 Committee Decision* discussed in Section V of this report. In addition, these proposals would require WTO Members to apply the same criteria and procedures for accrediting or otherwise approving domestic and foreign conformity assessment bodies to test and certify products for its market and to accept test results performed by competent facilities outside the Member's territory.

The U.S. proposal on electronic goods also seeks to commit WTO Members to one of two forms of conformity assessment procedures in the areas of electrical safety and electro-magnetic compatibility – third party certification or a suppliers' declaration of conformity. The proposal would establish disciplines for both types of procedures that ensure, for example, any product testing a Member requires can be performed in the exporting country and that U.S. testing and certification bodies are treated no less favorably than conformity assessment bodies located in the territories of other WTO Members.

Finally, the U.S. proposal on autos seeks to encourage Members to (a) participate in the work of international standardizing bodies as a way of harmonizing technical regulations and conformity assessment procedures for those products; (b) consider other Members' automotive technical regulations and conformity assessment procedures when they determine that there is a need to regulate and explain any proposed deviations in substance from relevant international standards; and (c) provide at least 18 months for producers to comply with a new technical regulation that would require substantial change in automobile design or technology.

The Emerging Technologies Interagency Policy Committee

The United States recognizes the critical importance of enhanced interagency coordination in developing regulatory policy for emerging technologies. Emerging technologies promise to have significant scientific, economic, and perhaps societal impacts because of their potential to revolutionize fields as varied as materials science, electronics, medicine, communications, agriculture, and energy. Rapid scientific and technological advances in these fields are resulting in a variety of new products and processes with unique and transformational characteristics. But full realization of the economic and public benefits of these applications will require open consideration of policy questions with the full range of stakeholders, including governments, industry, non-governmental organizations, academia, and the public.

As a result, in 2010 the Administration formed the Emerging Technologies Interagency Policy Coordination Committee (ETIPC), part of an effort to give special attention to technologies so new—such as nanotechnology and synthetic biology—that their policy implications are still being gauged. Created jointly by the White House Office of Science and Technology Policy, OMB's Office of Information and Regulatory Affairs, and USTR, the ETIPC consists of assistant secretary-level representatives from about 20 Federal agencies. The ETIPC complements the work of the TPSC and the National Science and Technology Council, by providing a forum for appropriate and timely consideration of a broad range of policy questions and to coordinate positions that Federal agencies may take when engaging on these issues internationally. From a trade perspective, ETIPC will help the United States engage in regulatory cooperation activities with trading partners, with a view to avoiding the creation of unnecessary divergences in regulation and the creation of unnecessary technical barriers to trade in emerging technologies.

At the first meeting of the Committee in May 2010, the co-chairs outlined several guiding principles for the group's work, including the Administration's commitment to scientific integrity, innovation, and open government, ensuring that the benefits of regulation justify its costs, and using risk-benefit-based oversight mechanisms that ensure safety without stifling innovation, stigmatizing emerging technologies, or creating trade barriers.

X.   Trends in 2010

The U.S. government actively seeks to prevent and eliminate unnecessary technical barriers to trade by participating in a variety of venues and on many different levels. The preceding sections of this report reviewed U.S. government engagement in bilateral and multilateral venues on specific trade concerns and on systemic issues. Section X provides a summary of many of the specific concerns of the United States with standards-related activities in specific countries. This section reviews trends that appear across various U.S. trading partners' markets, as well as standards-related systemic issues, that can significantly affect the ability of U.S. businesses and producers to access foreign markets.

Regulatory Measures on Goods with Cryptographic Capabilities

A number of U.S. trading partners, including China, India, and the Russian Federation, have adopted problematic measures that block or restrict U.S. exports of products with cryptographic capabilities for commercial use. As an increasing number of products for commercial use are being designed with cryptographic capabilities to protect data integrity and confidentiality, these measures have the potential to significantly impede trade in a wide range of industrial products and systems. For example, China requires U.S. companies to provide their source codes as a condition for U.S. companies to market their products. Likewise, China, India, and Russia all require U.S. companies to partner with an indigenous company, thus jeopardizing business proprietary information, or require U.S. companies operating in these countries to use a country-specific cipher or algorithm. These measures tend to favor or require the use of specific domestic technologies that might not offer the strongest protection available, and may lead to the forced transfer of intellectual property. Consequently, these measures could stifle innovation and have a chilling effect on trade.

The United States is working with its trading partners to resolve these specific market access concerns and to ensure that other trading partners do not adopt similar troublesome practices in the future. U.S. officials will promote non-discrimination, the use of relevant international standards as a basis for regulation, and transparency and predictability in the development and implementation of measures regarding goods with cryptographic capabilities. Further, the United States is evaluating other opportunities to collaborate with its trading partners to help prevent the spread of problematic practices in the encryption sphere, including through the TPP negotiations.

Mandatory Biotech Labeling

A growing number of markets around the world require or have proposed mandatory retail labeling for food products that contain or are derived from biotechnology. Details, as well as implementation, of the regimes vary from market to market. However, the mandatory nature of these regimes has impeded, and in some cases, completely blocked U.S. exports of such food products to several countries. Some of the countries imposing mandatory biotech labeling requirements include Australia, Brazil, China, EU Member States, Indonesia, Japan, Korea, Malaysia, New Zealand, Peru, Russia, Saudi Arabia, Turkey, Ukraine, Thailand, Taiwan, and Vietnam. These measures pose a significant problem for U.S. agricultural exports as a result of the widespread use of biotechnology to produce corn, cotton, and soybeans, as well as food produced or processed from these crops in the United States. In fact, biotechnology crops represent a significant portion of U.S. agricultural exports, totaling $98.6 billion in 2009. Mandatory biotechnology labeling measures in Korea, Turkey, and Vietnam are discussed in greater detail in Section X.

Mandatory labeling of food products containing or derived from biotechnology has a negative impact on U.S. exports for many different reasons. First, mandatory labeling affects consumer impressions of a product subject to the labeling requirement. The fact that certain trading partners apply mandatory labeling requirements solely to products containing or derived from biotechnology creates the impression that these products are somehow different from or less safe than similar food that is not labeled. Second, mandatory biotechnology labeling increases costs for consumers and industry stakeholders that buy food produced using biotechnology. Third, many countries lack the infrastructure or mechanisms to implement and enforce their mandatory biotech labeling requirements in a consistent and transparent manner, which further compounds the negative impact on trade.

In many markets, the combined effect of these problems has caused companies to reformulate their products to eliminate the use of ingredients containing or derived from biotechnology. The additional costs of searching for alternative ingredients, some of which may be expensive or scarce, are often ultimately passed on to the consumer.

The United States will continue to raise trade-related concerns with mandatory biotechnology labeling regimes in 2011.

Recognition of Conformity Assessment Bodies

Last year's report included an illustrative list of conformity assessment barriers that U.S. exporters and conformity assessment service providers face. For a full description of these, and other similar barriers, see pages 52-56 of the *2010 TBT Report*.

U.S. officials continue to believe that conformity assessment barriers are a critical issue, and, as a result, the United States is devoting substantial resources to addressing these matters on a country-specific and systemic basis. These efforts produced some notable successes in 2010. For example, in an exchange of letters with the United States, Mexico recognized that, for certain electrical products, demonstrating compliance with U.S. electrical safety requirements was sufficient for these products to be granted access to the Mexican market without additional testing or certification in Mexico. This issue is discussed in greater detail in the Mexico section of this report.

Other challenges remain. For example, the China section of this report illustrates efforts by the U.S. Department of Commerce to resolve practical problems facing U.S. industry with respect to compliance with China's compulsory certification requirements. Likewise, the Korea section details efforts made by U.S. officials to urge Korea to liberalize further its conformity assessment regime, using recent successes with lithium-ion batteries and energy efficiency as a template. U.S. officials have also redoubled their efforts to target conformity assessment barriers in the context of the TPP negotiations.

Distilled Spirits Regulation

Barriers for distilled spirits have created significant standards-related trade problems for U.S. exporters. For example, the EU maintains a three-year minimum aging requirement for whiskey, prohibiting U.S. whiskey products that are aged for a shorter period from being sold or from being labeled as "whiskey" in the EU market. The EU's aging requirement is based on the climatic conditions in Scotland and Ireland and thus may be appropriate for the production of Scotch and Irish Whiskies. However, this aging period is not appropriate for whiskey produced in other climatic conditions, such as those in Kentucky, Tennessee, Indiana, and other U.S. states where less aging is required to achieve the same result. Further, recent advances in barrel technology have enabled U.S. micro-distillers to reduce the aging time for whiskey produced in the United States even further, which also demonstrates the inapplicability of a mandatory three-year aging requirement for whiskey.

The EU's policy on distilled spirits also adversely affects U.S. exports to other markets that are following the EU's lead and adopting similar policies. Israel, for example, recently adopted the same minimum aging requirement for blended whiskeys as the EU – even though Israel does not produce whiskey – and Colombia is considering doing the same. Colombia also is proposing that brandy be aged using the solera method, a system of aging that was developed in Europe and is not widely used in the United States. If Colombia adopts this policy, it could significantly restrict exports to Colombia of U.S. brandy.

Colombia has proposed requirements for other distilled spirits that could impede U.S. exports, including quality and identity requirements for vodka, gin, rum, and whiskey. In particular, Colombia is proposing to define these products based primarily on whether they meet certain analytical parameters for alcohol content, congener levels, and other factors. These definitions would differ significantly from the practice followed by North American and European regulators. North American and European definitions rely primarily on differences in the raw materials used, and production processes. If Colombia adopts this proposal, it could effectively bar some U.S. spirits from the Colombian market, such as those with alcohol content levels that fall above or below the ranges specified in the proposed Colombian requirements.

Vietnam has proposed setting maximum limits on aldehydes in distilled spirits – a policy that could impact U.S. distilled spirit exports to that country. Aldehydes are naturally occurring substances, and therefore are present in many distilled spirits. In addition, there is no widely-accepted scientific or technical basis for the limits on aldehyde content. The United States, along with the EU, raised concerns about this issue with Vietnam, and were successful in persuading Vietnam to drop this policy for all distilled spirits.

In 2010, U.S. producers continued to voice concerns about many other labeling requirements for alcoholic beverages that appear to lack a valid scientific basis. For example, U.S. producers raised concerns about Brazil's proposed labeling requirement for distilled spirits, Thailand's warning label proposal for all alcoholic beverages, and a similar proposal by Kenya. The United States is investigating these policies and will engage with these governments to encourage them to drop or modify their proposals.

From a broader standpoint, numerous countries are adopting policies that require suppliers to develop country-specific labels for spirits and other products, and these countries are requiring that this designation be made on a permanent label that is affixed in the country of export instead of the importing country. The United States is concerned about the manner in which this requirement is being imposed and the associated costs. In addition, it is not clear whether this requirement will diminish counterfeiting, the purported objective of many countries. As such, U.S. officials are evaluating opportunities to address this issue on a systemic basis, including through the TPP negotiations.

More details can be found in the country reports on Brazil, Colombia, Thailand, and Vietnam in Section X.

Organic Product Standards

Foreign regulations governing organic products can make exporting U.S. organic products a costly and burdensome endeavor and, in some instances, prohibitively so. In the organics sector, the United States has negotiated three types of agreements with major trading partners in an attempt to facilitate trade in organic products:

- Under a "recognition agreement," an importing country agrees to recognize USDA's National Organic Program (NOP) to accredit agents within the United States to certify products as organic under the importing country's requirements. The United States has negotiated such an agreement with the EU. Similarly, USDA has recognized foreign conformity assessment bodies to accredit certifying agents in other countries (Denmark, India, Israel, Japan, New Zealand, and the United Kingdom) to certify products as organic under the NOP.

- Under an "equivalency arrangement," the United States and another country agree to allow some or all products produced and certified to the exporting country's organic requirements to be sold as organic in the importing country. The United States concluded its first equivalency arrangement with Canada, the largest U.S. organics trading partner, in 2009.

- Under an "export arrangement," U.S. organics producers can sell their products as organic in another market (*e.g.,* Japan, Taiwan), provided that their products meet specific requirements of the importing country.

These efforts have been highly effective in facilitating trade in organic products. However, in some instances it has not been possible to bridge some, or all, of the differences between U.S. and foreign organics requirements using these tools.

For example, Japan's zero tolerance policy for pesticide and herbicide residues on organic products limits U.S. organics exports to Japan. Japan's ban on alkali extracted humic acid, a substance that USDA permits for use on U.S. organic crops, also limits U.S. organics exports. Similarly, Korea's zero tolerance policy for adventitious presence of biotechnology content in organic products limits U.S. organics exports. If Korea does not adopt regulations allowing it to negotiate one or more of the arrangements outlined above, U.S. organics exports to Korea could be further restricted beginning in January 2013.

U.S. officials continue to engage with trading partners in an attempt to resolve these issues and to prevent new issues from arising. In May 2010, the United States and the EU began negotiations on a possible equivalency arrangement. The United States also hopes to begin positive engagement with Korea on an equivalency arrangement, following a successful effort to persuade Korea to allow U.S. organics products to remain in its market at least through January 2013. The United States is also investigating concerns raised by U.S. producers regarding China's organic standards.

Formula Disclosure Requirements

During 2010, many countries began requiring the disclosure of confidential business information as a condition of entry for food products into their markets. Some of these measures, such as those adopted by Brazil, Indonesia, and Japan, require that labels not only list a product's ingredients but also the percentages for each such ingredient. Other countries, such as Argentina, Chile, China, Turkey, and Venezuela, adopted measures that require companies to disclose a product's precise recipe or formula. Ecuador has proposed adopting a similar requirement.

In the United States, food containers must include nutritional labels that list ingredients in the order of their amounts in the product, but not to disclose the exact percentages or the formula. While some countries may require additional disclosures with the goals of ensuring the quality and safety of imported food products, other food safety and quality assurance mechanisms are available that can achieve the same objectives without compromising proprietary formulas. U.S. officials will continue to work bilaterally and in the TBT Committee to protect U.S. food industry's proprietary business information and intellectual property and to provide trading partners, as needed, with suggested alternative measures to ensure product safety and quality.

Issues Related to Trade in Halal Products

U.S. industry continues to face market access barriers for halal products. While the Codex *General Guidelines for Use of the Term "Halal"*[39] are helpful in setting out basic principles, governments have established halal standards that vary significantly based on which of the four predominant Islamic schools of thought a country embraces. U.S. industry has encountered difficulties in exporting halal products because of differences in how countries regulate slaughtering, handling and transportation, labeling, and certification for halal purposes, as well as when governments exceed the Codex halal guidelines.

As one example, Malaysia has adopted a standard that would require halal food to be processed in dedicated halal facilities, whereas the Codex standard recognizes food as halal if it is processed on a dedicated line within a facility that produces non-halal products. Likewise, Indonesia shut down imports of U.S. poultry last year by abruptly terminating its recognition of existing halal certifiers and establishing a new list of certifiers without notice. Last year, Indonesia also attempted to apply halal standards to pharmaceuticals, over-the-counter medicines, and cosmetics, which could have resulted in a *de facto* ban on imports of certain varieties of these products that contain porcine or alcohol.

While some governments have attempted to frame their halal rules as a food safety issue, the United States has consistently viewed halal as a process/quality standard with no inherent food

---

[39] CAC/GL 24-1997

safety component. The U.S. view is supported by the Codex halal guidelines. The United States has used the WTO TBT Committee to raise its concerns with halal implementation issues, and has been successful in many cases. For example, the United States persuaded Indonesia to withdraw its attempt to apply halal standards to pharmaceuticals, over-the-counter medicines, and cosmetics in 2010. In addition, U.S. efforts ensured that Indonesia recognized four U.S. poultry certifiers as halal certifiers for U.S. poultry, reopening the market to U.S. halal poultry products. The United States is continuing to engage with Indonesia and Malaysia on these issues in 2011, as well as with other countries that maintain or are considering adopting similar requirements.

Problematic Documentation Requirements

Across industry sectors, U.S. exporters have faced documentation requirements as a condition for market entry. These requirements may raise costs for U.S. exporters or serve as a barrier to entry. For example:

- Brazil, China, Israel, Japan, Russia, Switzerland, Thailand, Turkey, Venezuela, among other countries, require certificates of analysis from U.S. exporters of wine, even when exporters already hold certificates verifying that their wines conform to both U.S. and the importing country's standards. Often a country will require that these certificates be an original document issued by U.S. government officials or officially accredited organizations from the country of importation. In Russia, for example, a U.S. winery may be required to pay as much as $5,000 for the two certificates required for hygiene and the *Gosstandart Russia* Certificates of Conformity to wine standards.

- U.S. industry has raised concerns that countries such as Chile, Costa Rica, the Dominican Republic, Guatemala, and Indonesia require some U.S. exporters (*e.g.,* of medical devices, pharmaceuticals, and cosmetics products) to "legalize" their documentation, oftentimes through the local embassy of the country of importation (which charges a fee), before filing applications for approval. This can add significant costs to the process of exporting. In addition, U.S. industry alleges that Peru requires documentation submitted to gain approvals for pharmaceuticals to be provided in a "Peru specific format" even when the information has been submitted to other countries and approved in the same format, leading to delays in approval of Peruvian applications.

- Countries such as China and Korea require medical device producers to submit evidence of "prior approval" that the device offered for export has been approved in the country of manufacture or origin. This requirement adds costs and delays to the approval process. In some cases, the product has been designed exclusively for export. In those cases, it is inappropriate to require the exporter to seek approval from its home country.

- Brazil requires medical device producers to submit business proprietary economic data (*e.g.,* prices in other markets, distributor mark-ups, advertising/promotion budgets) as a condition for registering or re-registering their products, even though such data may not exist or is unrelated to medical device safety or efficacy. In the process of purportedly clarifying Brazil's procedures for registering medical devices, Brazil's regulator posted business proprietary economic data on its web site, contrary to assurances it had provided to U.S. industry that it would not do so.

The U.S. government works to resolve these issues as they arise in individual cases through the TBT Committee and bilateral engagement. The United States also looks for opportunities to try and resolve these issues, or prevent their emergence, on a systemic basis. APEC is conducting work to promote streamlining of export certificate requirements for agricultural products consistent with Codex guidelines on official certificates for import and export. The TPP negotiations may present another such opportunity for the United States to make progress on this issue.

The Rise of "Voluntary" Measures as Trade Barriers

In various product sectors, U.S. trading partners have adopted measures that are technically voluntary, but which are applied in a manner that makes compliance mandatory. As a result, these policies are not governed by the strong disciplines on mandatory product standards and conformity assessment procedures included in the TBT Agreement. One way countries have avoided their obligations is by developing voluntary standards through procedures that exclude foreign stakeholders (a practice that the TBT Agreement does not prohibit for developing voluntary standards) and then later turning these voluntary standards into requirements (where it is prohibited). Even if foreign stakeholders are provided the opportunity to comment when the government proposes to convert a voluntary standard into a technical requirement, it is often too late to shape the measure and avoid erecting a barrier to trade. For example:

- Korea's Energy Management Corporation (KEMCO) only certifies one type of thin film solar panel – the type that Korean producers manufacture – as meeting its version of the International Electrotechnical Commission standard. While compliance with that standard is not technically required for sale of solar panels in the Korean market, a company will not be commercially viable in Korea without KEMCO certification. As a result, U.S. solar panel producers that make different kinds of thin film panels find themselves locked out of the Korean market.

- The EU often issues voluntary standards (*e.g.,* for lawnmowers and pressure vessels, among other products) and then later clarifies that there is a "presumption of compliance" with a mandatory requirement if these voluntary standard are followed. Because the EU's voluntary standards are developed in a system where each EU Member State has a vote and U.S. companies without a European presence are excluded, this puts U.S. companies at a disadvantage because the standard often does not reflect their input.

- Japan issues voluntary guidelines for advanced safety features in automobiles. Although compliance with these guidelines is *not* technically mandatory, it is expected that industry will comply, and therefore the guidelines are *de facto* mandatory. However, Japan relies on the fact that the guidance is not formally binding to avoid complying with WTO notification and other notice and comment procedures.

- The organic and halal standards that many governments have adopted are technically voluntary, but they often serve to preclude U.S. products from entering the market. For example, when Malaysia put in place a voluntary standard that did not allow for halal products to be manufactured on a dedicated line within a facility that also produces non-halal products, many U.S. poultry and beef producers were effectively excluded from the Malaysian market. This is because Malaysia bans imports of non-halal poultry and beef products and it is often too costly for U.S. producers to set up separate production facilities for those products.

As with the other issues identified in this section of the report, the United States works to resolve issues concerning voluntary standards through the TBT Committee and bilateral engagement as they arise in individual markets. The United States is also seeking to address these issues on a systemic basis as over 20 percent of the specific trade concerns that WTO Members raised in the TBT Committee in 2010 related to "standards." Currently, U.S. officials are seeking opportunities to tackle the issue of voluntary standards in the NAMA and the TPP negotiations. The United States will also look to address this issue through the TBT Committee during the upcoming Sixth Triennial Review of the TBT Agreement.

XI. Country Reports

Background on Trade Concerns Contained in the Country Reports

This section contains individual country reports detailing TBT barriers encountered by U.S. stakeholders. The measures and practices the country reports identify raise significant trade concerns, and, in some instances, give rise to questions concerning whether a trading partner is complying with its obligations under trade agreements to which the United States is a party.[40] The decisions on which issues to include resulted from an interagency process that incorporated the expertise of a variety of government agencies.

While the tools used to address TBT barriers vary depending on the particular circumstances, in all instances, USTR's goal remains the same: to work as vigorously and expeditiously as possible to resolve the issue in question. As reflected in the country reports, in many instances USTR seeks to resolve specific concerns through dialogue with the pertinent trading partner – either bilaterally or through multilateral fora – and working collaboratively to obtain changes that result in improved market access for U.S. exporters.

The *TBT Report* provides more focused and structured reporting on country-specific standards-related issues compared to what appeared in prior NTE reports. Conversely, some prior NTE reports may have included standards-related issues that USTR has not included in the *TBT Report*.

In response to USTR's outreach in compiling this report, stakeholders raised a number of new standards-related concerns. In several cases, USTR lacked sufficient information about those concerns at the time of publication to include them in this report. For purposes of this report, USTR included measures and practices about which USTR is well informed; USTR continues, however, to gather information about others. Accordingly, the omission of any issue in this report should not be taken to mean that USTR will not pursue it, as appropriate, with the trading partners concerned, in the same manner as those listed below.

It is important to note that there are fewer country-specific trade issues set out in the *2011 TBT Report* than in the *2010 TBT Report* because the 2010 TBT Report included some issues that the United States successfully addressed last year, including several trade issues with China (cotton registration requirements, excessive packaging requirements, and Green Dam), Korea (WIPI requirement for cell phones, cosmetics approval process, and testing requirements for energy efficiency and lithium ion batteries); Brazil (quality and identity standards for distilled spirits), and Israel (auto parts labeling requirement). The United States also resolved issues involving conformity assessment procedures for children's products in Brazil and Malaysia, and Ecuador's conformity assessment procedures for industrial products.

---

[40] Nothing in this report should be construed as a legal determination that a measure included in the report falls within the scope of any particular WTO Agreement (*e.g.*, whether the measure is subject to the TBT as opposed to the SPS Agreement).

Since the resolution of these issues was discussed in the *2010 TBT Report*, they are no longer included in this section. However, the United States continues to monitor these issues closely to ensure that they do not re-emerge as problems for U.S. industry. Similarly, an analysis of the country sections of the *2011 TBT Report* demonstrates that numerous other issues were recently resolved or are on a path to resolution. Despite these successes, U.S. exporters still face a variety of specific trade concerns as a result of measures adopted or proposed in the 17 countries and the EU as described in the pages that follow.

Argentina

Bilateral Engagement

The United States raises TBT matters with Argentina both bilaterally and during meetings of the TBT Committee.

Toys – Testing and Accreditation Requirements

On June 4, 2008, Argentina's Ministry of Health (MoH) issued Resolution 583/2008, limiting the amount of phthalates that toys and other children's articles may contain. While the regulation applies to all such products, it only calls for imported products to be tested for compliance. In addition, the resolution initially required imported toys and children's articles to be accompanied by a technical report from the Argentina's Center for Research and Technological Development for the Plastics Industry (INTI). Importers could not substitute technical reports from laboratories outside Argentina.

U.S. industry raised concerns regarding the resolution. In particular, U.S. industry expressed concern that there would be significant delays, costs, and burdens in exporting toys and children's articles to Argentina based on INTI's limited capacity to perform the required testing and the inability to test these products in the country of production. After the resolution was implemented, some U.S. stakeholders experienced significant delays in exporting toys to Argentina. One company reported that complying with the in-country test requirement added more than 90 days to the process of placing its products on the market.

The United States raised the matter with Argentina during TBT Committee meetings in 2009, and MoH subsequently revised its requirements. Revisions made in December 2009 and May 2010 had the effect of allowing suppliers to export toys and children's products to Argentina without a test report from INTI if the products were accompanied by: (1) a sworn statement affirming that the products meet Argentine product safety requirements; and (2) written proof issued by INTI that samples of the products had been received and were in the process of being analyzed. U.S. industry believed this procedure would reduce delays, but indicated that Argentina should consider additional revisions, such as recognizing laboratories outside of Argentina and expanding laboratory capacity in Argentina to ensure that producers could obtain test results in a prompt fashion.

The United States continued to press Argentina on this issue at the April 2010 meeting of the U.S. – Argentina Bilateral Council on Trade and Investment. In response, MoH adopted Resolution 806/2010 in May 2010, which further revised its testing requirements. This resolution's stated objective is "to expand the coverage of laboratories for phthalates testing by extending this responsibility to other competent and accordingly certified institutions." The resolution provides for the Argentine Organization for Accreditation (OAA), an ILAC-MRA signatory body, to accredit foreign laboratories. While this resolution appears to be another positive development, OAA has yet to recognize any laboratories located outside of Argentina to conduct the required testing, including bodies that are accredited by other ILAC-MRA signatories. Accordingly, the United States will continue to raise this issue with Argentina in 2011.

Brazil

Bilateral Engagement

The United States and Brazil discuss TBT-related matters at various bilateral fora, including the Bilateral Consultative Mechanism (led by Brazil's Ministry of External Relations and USTR), the Commercial Dialogue (led by Brazil's Ministry of Development, Industry, and Commerce and the U.S. Department of Commerce), and the Economic Partnership Dialogue (led by Brazil's Ministry of External Relations and the U.S. Department of State). The United States also discusses TBT matters with Brazil during TBT Committee meetings and bilaterally on the margins of these meetings.

Alcoholic Beverages – Labeling Requirements

In October 2009, Brazil notified the WTO of proposed revisions to its regulations governing the labeling of beverages and products of acetic fermentations. During meetings of the TBT Committee in June and November 2010, the United States raised concerns that some of the proposed revisions could potentially prohibit imports of specific U.S.–origin, internationally-traded spirits. Specifically, the United States expressed concerns with: (1) a prohibition on the use of abbreviations for common terms on labels; (2) a requirement that product names be printed on the main label in bold face and upper case letters; (3) a requirement that a large decal be placed on the label including the importer's registration number; and (4) a prohibition on the use of certain expressions on labels (such as "home-made", "hand-crafted", "reserve" and "special reserve"), even if these are associated with a company's name or trademark.

The United States also asked Brazil to clarify certain elements of its proposal, including: (1) whether the revised regulation would restrict the use of fanciful drawings and illustrations that are well-established elements of the trademark and clearly not intended to represent an ingredient of the spirit; (2) whether labels that display a drawing, figure, or illustration of any ingredient used to prepare the beverage must indicate all of the ingredients of animal or plant origin, regardless of quantity; and (3) the basis for requiring beverage cans to bear the statement *"This container must be washed prior to consumption."*

During the November 2010 TBT Committee meeting, Brazilian officials indicated the revised regulation would not restrict the use of fanciful drawings and illustrations of type the United States referred to and that Brazil would allow the use of abbreviations for common terms. However, Brazil did not provide these clarifications in writing. Brazilian officials also noted that Brazil continues to review the proposed revision and will notify the WTO of any further changes. Thus far, U.S. industry has not reported any disruption of U.S. distilled spirits shipments to Brazil. The United States continues to monitor the situation closely.

Medical Devices – Inspection Requirements

Resolution 25, which Brazil notified to the WTO on May 18, 2009, requires ANVISA (Brazil's medical device inspection agency) to inspect facilities that produce certain "high risk" medical devices to be sold in the Brazilian market by May 22, 2010. The United States does not contest Brazil's right to inspect U.S. facilities; in fact, the U.S. Food and Drug Administration (FDA) maintains analogous authority to conduct inspections of Brazilian and other foreign facilities. However, the United States has been concerned that ANVISA would not have sufficient resources to inspect all overseas facilities that ship these devices to the Brazilian market by the May 22, 2010 deadline, potentially disrupting hundreds of millions of dollars in U.S. exports and jeopardizing the adequate supply of essential medical devices to the Brazilian market.

In late 2009 and early 2010, the U.S. government and U.S. industry representatives engaged with ANVISA in an attempt to clarify the inspection requirements and seek assurances from Brazil that trade in medical devices would not be disrupted after the deadline if ANVISA could not complete all of the inspections (and related registrations) in time. In response, Brazil clarified that class I medical devices (*e.g.,* tongue depressors, bedpans) and class II devices (*e.g.,* powered wheelchairs, surgical drapes) would be exempted from the inspection requirement, and that ANVISA's inspections would apply only to the last place of manufacture (as opposed to all the supplier facilities). Additionally, Brazil indicated that only plants manufacturing devices subject to re-registrations or new registrations would need to be inspected by May 22, 2010; other products could remain on the Brazilian market after the deadline pending an inspection.

Despite this progress, problems remain. In October 2010, ANVISA issued Technical Note No. 001/2010/GGTPS/*ANVISA (Requirement of Good Manufacturing Practices and Control Certificate)*, which will require GMP inspections and registration processes to be conducted consecutively for products filed with ANVISA after the deadline instead of allowing these processes to occur simultaneously. U.S. industry is concerned that this change will delay entry of new medical devices by over a year given the number of inspections already pending with ANVISA. The United States will continue to monitor the situation closely in 2011 to ensure that U.S. exports are not disrupted.

Medical Devices – Data Requirements for Registration

Resolution 185 of 2001, which sets out ANVISA's registration requirements for medical devices, requires manufacturers to submit detailed economic data, including confidential and proprietary information. The data requirement does not appear to fulfill a legitimate objective related to evaluating medical device safety or efficacy. As explained in last year's *TBT Report*, ANVISA in 2009 published a resolution clarifying the registration requirements, which was welcomed by U.S. and industry officials. Around the same time, Brazil also committed to U.S. industry that it would not publish any confidential or proprietary information.

On September 14, 2010, ANVISA unexpectedly published company-specific pricing data that individual U.S. producers had supplied. The United States raised concerns regarding ANVISA's action with Brazilian officials on the margins of the TBT Committee meeting in

November 2010. The United States continues to urge ANVISA to remove the proprietary data from its website. At the same time, the United States is working with U.S. industry to develop a methodology for displaying the data where needed while also protecting the confidentiality of information manufacturers provide in the registration process.

Telecommunications – Acceptance of Test Results

Brazil's National Telecommunications Regulatory Agency (ANATEL) does not accept test data generated outside Brazil, except in cases where the equipment is too physically large or costly to transport. Accordingly, U.S. suppliers must submit virtually all of their information technology and telecommunications equipment for testing to laboratories located in Brazil before it can be placed on the Brazilian market. This requirement results in redundant testing to be conducted, and consequently, both higher costs and delayed time to market in Brazil.

During 2010, the United States continued to urge Brazil to implement the CITEL (Inter-American Telecommunication Commission) MRA. Brazil has not agreed to do so, and the United States will continue to advocate for this position in 2011. If Brazil implemented the CITEL MRA it would benefit Brazilian suppliers seeking to sell into the U.S. market by enabling them to use test results from laboratories located in Brazil to certify that their telecommunications products meet FCC requirements.

Toys and Children's Articles – Conformity Assessment Procedures

In past years, U.S. industry raised concerns about a measure that Brazil's National Institute of Metrology, Standardization, and Industrial Quality (INMETRO) proposed to amend Brazil's existing conformity assessment procedures for toys and children's articles. The measure would have permitted foreign manufacturers to test their toys for compliance with Brazilian toy safety requirements in the country of manufacture. However, this proposal would have required imported toys already tested abroad to undergo a second round of testing in Brazil, while only requiring domestically-produced toys to be tested once. In addition, the industry was concerned about Brazil's proposed procedures for placing INMETRO conformity assessment seals on conforming products in Brazil. In particular, U.S. producers requested to use either the System 5 ("Compliance Imprint Certification Model") or System 7 ("Lot Certification Model") conformity assessment procedures for their products, similar to Brazilian producers.

During meetings of the TBT Committee in 2009, the United States, joined by the EU, Thailand, and China, noted that it strongly shares Brazil's objective of protecting children from exposure to potentially dangerous substances in toys and other children's articles, but questioned the basis for Brazil's requirement that imported toys would be subject to two sets of tests, while domestic toys would only be subject to one. As noted in last year's report, in September 2009 INMETRO announced several improvements to its conformity assessment procedures to address some of the concerns that were raised. Most notably, these improvements proposed to: (1) eliminate the second test requirement on imports; (2) allow laboratories accredited by an ILAC MRA signatory to conduct the testing in certain circumstances; (3) provide foreign producers with the option of importing under System 5 or System 7; and (4) permit foreign producers using System 5 to add the INMTERO conformity assessment seal at the place of manufacture instead of in Brazil. In early November 2009, INMETRO published a revised measure incorporating these improvements and notified it to the WTO. Brazil indicated that the measure would take effect on May 22, 2010. The United States welcomed the new measure.

In early May 2010, the United States posed additional questions about how the new system would operate in practice to ensure that it would not create unnecessary export barriers for U.S. industry. INMETRO replied to these questions and extended the implementation period an additional 5 months to October 29, 2010. The United States has not received any reports of export issues arising from Brazil's implementation of the new measure, but will continue to monitor the situation.

Products of Animal Origin – Labeling Registration Requirement

In August and September 2010, Brazil notified the WTO of proposed changes to its labeling registration form for products of animal origin. Brazil's new registration form requires the health or veterinary authority of the exporting country to certify that an exporter's establishment is "in compliance" with Brazilian standards and legislation. The United States does not consider it appropriate for governments to condition access to their markets for animal products on a certification of this nature. Further, Brazil's requirement causes particular concerns for U.S. industry because U.S. health and veterinary authorities are not authorized under federal law to attest that a U.S. production facility complies with a foreign country's market standards or legislation.

In September 2010, the U.S. government and U.S. industry submitted comments to Brazil regarding the proposed measure, and U.S. officials raised the issue with Brazil during the November 2010 TBT Committee meeting. Brazil provided a response to U.S. comments, which U.S. officials are reviewing. The United States will continue to monitor this issue and ensure that Brazil's measure does not disrupt trade in products of animal origin.

Wine – Certification

In December 2009, Brazil notified the WTO that it had eliminated its requirement for wineries to register the Brazilian government, a step that will reduce costs for U.S. exporters. At the same time, Brazil instituted a new certificate of origin and product analysis requirement for imported wine products, which would raise costs. During 2010, U.S. industry informed the U.S. Alcohol and Tobacco Tax and Trade Bureau (TTB) that Brazilian Customs had held up several U.S. wine shipments on the ground that the shipments did not comply with this new requirement.

The United States raised concerns with Brazil about this issue at the TBT Committee meetings throughout 2010. At these meetings, the United States pointed out that this new requirement is unnecessary and duplicative since the TTB already issues certificates of analysis, origin, free sale, and typicity for U.S. wines. The United States is continuing to work to resolve this issue and to ensure that U.S. wine exports do not face any additional market access restrictions in Brazil.

Beverage Registration

In December 2009, Brazil notified the WTO of a proposed measure that would require the government of each exporting country to provide a list of approved production facilities for non-alcoholic beverages, distilled spirits, and malt beverages as well as a list of laboratories that would test these products to ensure they met Brazil's requirements for import. On September 14, 2010, the United States submitted comments to Brazil on its proposed measure, indicating that it would be impossible for the U.S. government to comply with Brazil's proposed requirement for non-alcoholic beverages because the United States does not accredit organizations and laboratories for the testing or export of non-alcoholic beverages.

These new requirements, which took effect September 28, 2010, have already adversely affected U.S. exports. Brazilian customs officials detained at least four shipments of U.S.-produced vegetable juices and sauces in late 2010. While U.S. officials at the U.S. Agricultural Trade Office in Brasilia were able to secure the release of these products, these actions do not provide a basis for a viable long-term solution to the problem.

In an effort to secure a more permanent solution, the United States raised concerns regarding this issue with Brazil bilaterally in November 2010. In particular, the United States asked Brazil to indicate how it will allow imports from countries that do not maintain a list of government-approved laboratories and to explain whether it maintains a similar list for domestic companies. In response to U.S. concerns, Brazil requested the United States to propose an alternate certification procedure. The United States continues to press Brazil for specific responses to the U.S. questions while discussing potential practical ways forward with U.S. industry.

China

Bilateral Engagement

The United States and China regularly engage on TBT-related issues through the U.S.-China Joint Commission on Commerce and Trade (JCCT) and bilaterally on a case-by-case basis as specific market access issues arise. The JCCT, which was established in 1983, is the main forum for addressing bilateral trade matters and promoting commercial opportunities between the United States and China. The JCCT has played a key role in helping to resolve bilateral TBT issues, including those related to medical device recalls and registration, certification of IT products, and cotton registration requirements.

At the October 2009 JCCT meeting, the United States and China agreed to convene a public-private meeting on standards and conformity assessment procedures to increase collaboration on standards and conformity issues. This meeting was subsequently held in the first quarter of 2010. The JCCT has also played a key role in helping to resolve bilateral TBT issues, including those related to medical device recalls, registration and certification requirements for information technology (IT) products, and cotton registration requirements. Also, as agreed during the 2009 JCCT meeting, the U.S. Department of Commerce, together with the Standardization Administration of China (SAC), co-hosted a standards roundtable on energy efficiency and new energy on September 29, 2010 in Beijing.

USTR is continuing to monitor closely China's development and use of standards and technical regulations in the IT sector, as discussed in more detail at pages 50-51 of the *2010 TBT Report*.

China Compulsory Certification (CCC) Requirements – Conformity Assessment Procedures

Since 2003, China has required the China Compulsory Certification (CCC) mark to be applied to Chinese and foreign goods covering more than 159 product categories – including electrical machinery, IT equipment, household appliances, and their components. U.S. industry has raised concerns about multiple aspects of these requirements, including that they are particularly burdensome for SMEs because any applications for CCC mark exemptions must be submitted in China's Certification Accreditation Administration (CNCA) Beijing offices. The United States has also had longstanding concerns that China does not permit U.S. suppliers to use competent conformity assessment bodies (*e.g.*, testing laboratories, inspection bodies, and product certifiers) located outside China's territory to demonstrate that their products comply with CCC mark requirements. To date, CNCA has not accredited any U.S. conformity assessment body to test and certify products and inspect facilities for purposes of the CCC mark.

China's failure to accredit laboratories for testing, and to test or certify products for purposes of the CCC mark adversely impacts U.S. exports to China as at least 20 percent of U.S. exports to China must obtain the CCC mark prior to market entry. Because China will not accept testing and certification performed by U.S. conformity assessment bodies, U.S. exporters must submit their products to Chinese laboratories for tests that have already been performed abroad, resulting in greater expense and delayed access to China's market. In addition, because there is typically only one designated certification body in China authorized to perform testing, inspection, and certification for any given product, U.S. suppliers regularly report delays in marketing their products. Further, since Chinese conformity assessment bodies do not generally have a presence outside of China, U.S. companies exporting to China must: (1) arrange and fund travel by a Chinese inspection agent to perform pre-market inspections at the manufacturer's location in the United States; (2) submit to subsequent annual inspections after receiving authority to apply the CCC mark to their products; and (3) pay for their products to be tested and certified in China. U.S. industry also asserts that China's conformity assessment bodies often change their criteria without providing advance notice and an opportunity to comment.

In 2010, the United States continued to emphasize concerns to China regarding its CCC mark requirements. The United States, in collaboration with U.S. industry, organized a pair of cooperative roundtables with CNCA in 2010 to increase awareness and appreciation in China of U.S industry concerns regarding virtually every stage of China's complex and multifaceted CCC program, including: (1) transparency, procedural, and cost concerns associated with submitting U.S. manufacturing facilities to pre-market inspections by Chinese inspection agents; (2) issues related to shipping and arranging to have a product tested and certified in China; (3) additional requirements for type-approval requirements and provincial post-market inspections; and (4) the requirement of subsequent factory inspections to retain use of the CCC mark. The roundtables also provided opportunities for U.S. participants to glean additional information concerning how the CCC program operates, which will help support and inform the broader U.S. approach to addressing systemic trade concerns related to China's conformity assessment procedures.

In 2011, the United States will continue to work with China to find practical solutions to the concerns about CCC compliance issues. Among other suggestions, the United States will urge China to take positive, trade-facilitating steps to liberalize its approach to recognizing competent foreign conformity assessment bodies, such as by recognizing laboratories that have been accredited under an ILAC MRA or by IAF MLA signatories.

IT Products – Mandatory Testing and Certification

In August 2007, China notified to the WTO a series of thirteen proposed measures requiring certain IT products to be certified for information security functions. The proposed measures appeared to require testing and certification to certain Chinese national standards for information security which, in some areas, may differ from international standards used in the global market. In some cases, the Chinese standards require access to algorithms held by Chinese regulators, and it is unclear on what basis those algorithms will be made available. China's General Administration of Quality Supervision, Inspection and Quarantine (AQSIQ) indicated that the thirteen proposed measures would be mandatory for all covered products as of May 1, 2009.

The United States and other WTO Members expressed serious concerns to China about these proposed measures in numerous bilateral and multilateral meetings, and China eventually confirmed that the compulsory certification requirement will apply only when products are sold to government agencies, and not to state-owned enterprises or in other sectors of China's economy. This concession represented a significant reduction in the scope of the requirements from China's original plan. In October 2009, China also agreed to a dialogue with the United States regarding global best practices for trade in information security products.

In 2010, the United States continued to monitor potential Chinese activities in the information security sphere. When it became apparent that China's State Encryption Management Bureau was planning to revise its 1999 Regulations on Commercial Encryption Codes, the United States raised concerns in the TBT Committee, noting that should China's planned revision of these regulations expand their scope to more IT products, the impact of the encryption regulations would be felt across a broader swath of the global IT sector. U.S. officials also noted that such an expansion could create the sort of trade disruption that China's initial version of the encryption regulations engendered they were issued in 1999. Several months after releasing the initial version, China reduced the scope of the regulations to products whose core function is encryption. USTR will continue to monitor closely any developments in this area in 2011.

Medical Devices – Conformity Assessment Procedures

The United States has expressed concerns that China maintains two separate authorities — the State Food and Drug Administration (SFDA) and AQSIQ — to enforce regulations with similar, but not identical, requirements for selected medical devices. The potential overlapping and unclear delineation of responsibilities can result in additional and unnecessary regulatory procedures with no demonstrable public health benefit. For example, Decree 95, issued by AQSIQ in June 2007, would have imposed an onerous examination and supervision regime on imported medical devices, introducing additional testing and inspection redundancy to the certification schemes administered by SFDA and, in some cases, CNCA.

The United States, working closely with U.S. industry, has raised these concerns with China on multiple occasions, including at the JCCT. In November 2007, AQSIQ issued a notice suspending implementation of Decree 95. In a further step to streamline the registration process, in September 2008 SFDA and AQSIQ jointly announced that they would require only one test, one report, one fee, and one factory inspection for medical devices. Industry welcomed this commitment, projecting that by reducing redundancies this step could cut medical device approval times in half, which would provide U.S. industry with more timely access to China's medical device market.

In April 2009, SFDA circulated for public comment a draft measure intended to supersede the Administrative Measures on Medical Device Registration, originally issued in 2004, but did not notify the draft measure to the WTO. The United States subsequently expressed concerns about this draft measure in bilateral discussions with SFDA during the October 2009 JCCT meeting, and before the TBT Committee as part of China's Transitional Review Mechanism (TRM). Of particular concern was a proposal to require all medical devices to be registered in the country of export or the manufacturer's legal residence before they could be accepted for registration in China.

This requirement had the potential to block, or inordinately delay, sales of safe, high-quality medical devices to the Chinese market because manufacturers may decide not to seek to have their devices approved in the countries in which they are produced or in the producers' home countries for reasons unconnected with the quality or safety of their products. For example, producers may design particular medical devices specifically for patients in a third country, such as China, or may choose to produce them in a third country for export only. In these situations, a manufacturer would have no business reason to seek to have a particular device approved in its home country or the country of export and would likely forego that process in order to avoid the associated burdens of time and money.

Also in April 2009, AQSIQ circulated draft Regulations on the Recall of Defective Products, which would apply to medical devices. Given that China's Ministry of Health and SFDA had begun a process in 2008 to develop a recall system that would also cover medical devices, the United States became concerned about the possibility of redundant recall procedures. The United States raised its concerns in bilateral JCCT-related discussions, as well as during the WTO's China TRM process.

During the October 2009 JCCT meeting, China indicated that it would not require a medical device to be registered in the country of export or in the country of legal residence of the manufacturer as part of its prior approval process for medical devices. However, draft measures of the State Council on Supervision and Administration of Medical Devices issued in 2010 maintained the country of export registration requirement. In bilateral discussions with China during 2010, the United States continued to urge China to exclude the registration from its final measures. The United States will continue to press this issue during 2011.

In addition, China's continued failure to permit U.S. suppliers to use competent conformity assessment bodies (*e.g.*, testing laboratories, inspection bodies, or product certifiers) located outside China to demonstrate that their products comply with Chinese requirements negatively affects U.S. exports of medical devices to China. Since China will not accept testing and certification that the U.S. manufacturer or a U.S. conformity assessment body has conducted, U.S. medical device exporters must submit their products to Chinese laboratories for tests that have already been performed in the United States, resulting in greater expense and a longer time to market.

During the October 2009 JCCT meeting, China indicated that it would consider exempting medical devices from being tested in Chinese laboratories where manufacturers can demonstrate that their devices comply with relevant international standards. Based on information the U.S. government has received from industry stakeholders to date, however, it appears that China has not yet taken action to exempt such products from testing in Chinese laboratories. The United States will continue to press China on this issue in 2011.

Mobile Phones – WAPI Standard

In 2003, China issued two standards for encryption over wireless local area networks (WLANs), applicable to domestic and imported equipment containing WLAN technologies. Conformance to these standards was scheduled to become mandatory in 2004. The standards incorporated the WAPI encryption algorithm for secure communications. China sought to enforce the use of WAPI by mandating a particular algorithm (rather than mandating the need for encryption, and leaving the choice of the algorithm to market factors) and providing the necessary algorithm only to a limited number of Chinese companies. Had the standards become mandatory, U.S. and other foreign manufacturers would have been compelled to work with and through these companies, some of which were competitors, and provide them with their proprietary technical product specifications. Following high-level bilateral engagement, China agreed in April 2004 to postpone indefinitely implementing WAPI and to work within international standards processes in developing future wireless standards. This commitment led China to submit WAPI for consideration in ISO and IEC's Joint Technical Committee 1 (JTC1). In a 2006 ballot of ISO/IEC JTC1 members, the proposed WAPI amendment did not secure enough votes to be accepted as an ISO/IEC standard.

Concerns regarding WAPI re-emerged in 2009 as China moved forward with plans to require the WAPI standard to be used in mobile handsets, despite the growing commercial success of computer products in China that comply with the internationally recognized WiFi standard developed by the Institute of Electrical and Electronics Engineers (IEEE). Moreover, over the past several years, global mobile handset makers have increasingly added WLAN/Internet capability to their products consistent with the WiFi standard, thus expanding the use of WLAN equipment beyond laptops and home computers to mobile handsets. However, until recently (as noted below) China had not issued type approvals for handsets that connect to the Internet through WLAN equipment, and instead had only issued type approvals for handsets that connect to the Internet through cellular networks, a practice that has required foreign equipment makers to disable WLAN/Internet capability before their handsets could be marketed in China.

In 2009, as part of its plan for encouraging an aggressive roll-out of third generation (3G) mobile handsets by Chinese telecommunications operators, many of which employ Internet-enabled via WLAN networks, China established a process for approving hand-held wireless devices such as Internet-enabled cell phones and smart phones. During bilateral talks in 2009, China indicated to U.S. government officials that it would approve devices that use the WiFi standard, but only if those devices are also enabled with the WAPI standard. Chinese officials acknowledged that there is no published or written measure setting out this requirement and that China has not notified this requirement to the WTO. In 2010, the United States continued to urge China to publish the measure in draft form, notify it to the WTO, allow a meaningful time for comments, and take the comments into account in developing any final measure.

Patents Used in Chinese National Standards

In recent years, concerns have arisen regarding China's proposed treatment of patented technology in connection with domestic standards development processes. First, in late 2004, concerns arose after the Standardization Commission of China (SAC) issued draft *Provisional Regulations for National Standards Relating to Patents (Provisional Regulations)* and key Chinese government officials made public statements that appeared to contemplate compulsory licensing of patented technologies used as national standards in China.

In November 2009, SAC circulated a new draft of the *Provisional Regulations* for public comment. This draft measure would implement China's vision for a standards development process and establish the general principle that mandatory national standards should not incorporate patented technologies. However, when mandatory national standards incorporate patented technologies, the draft measure provides for the possibility of a compulsory license if a patent holder does not grant a royalty-free license. This differs from the typical practice of accredited standards developing organizations in other countries, which require disclosure of intellectual property in the standards development process and support "reasonable and nondiscriminatory" (RAND) licensing policies with respect to intellectual property that is incorporated into a standard. RAND policies require concerned patent right holders to make any intellectual property incorporated into the standards that these bodies develop available to all interested parties on RAND terms. Within the standards development process, licensing terms are typically negotiated between the right holder and parties interested in implementing the standards.

Second, in 2006, the Chinese government's Electronic Standardization Institute (CESI), a Chinese government entity, released draft intellectual property policy rules for standards-setting organizations (SSOs). These draft rules envisage Chinese government involvement in standard-setting processes, including a requirement that SSOs obtain government approval for patent claims. Such government involvement could be exercised in a way that affects private party transactions and could raise concerns under certain circumstances.

In January 2010, the China National Institute of Standardization (CNIS) solicited public comments on its notice titled "Disposal Rules for the Inclusion of Patents in National Standards." The "Disposal Rules" are the supporting documents for SAC's Provisional Regulations. In October 2010, CNIS finished the second draft of the Provisional Regulations, "Special Procedure on Standards Making—Inclusion of Patents in National Standards," and submitted them to SAC for review.

U.S. companies have expressed serious concerns regarding these proposals. The United States will continue to monitor how China treats intellectual property through its SSOs, including the development and finalization of CESI's rules, as well as the development of SAC's revised Provisional Regulations. In addition, the United States will discuss these issues with China in the JCCT Intellectual Property Rights (IPR) Working Group, where both sides have agreed to discuss related issues with participants from all relevant Chinese and U.S. agencies.

Colombia

<u>Bilateral Engagement</u>

The United States discusses TBT matters with Colombia during TBT Committee meetings and on the margins of these meetings.

<u>Distilled Spirits – Quality, Identity and Labeling Requirements</u>

The *2010 TBT Report* and Section IX of this report outline U.S. industry concerns about quality and identity requirements that Colombia proposed in 2009 for distilled spirits, including gin, rum, vodka, and whiskey. The U.S. government and U.S. industry raised this issue with Colombia at TBT Committee meetings, and Colombia responded by clarifying and adjusting its measure to address many of the concerns that were raised. For example, Colombia abandoned its proposal to require quality certificates for distilled spirits and removed a proposal to hold all parties in the production responsible for maintaining sanitary conditions for these products.

Although Colombia made positive modifications to its requirements, the United States continues to be concerned about certain proposed requirements that have not been withdrawn. For example, Colombia has not withdrawn a proposal to use analytical parameters related to the chemical composition of spirits, such as a limit on congeners and other naturally occurring constituents included in gin, vodka, and rum. This policy could bar some U.S. spirits from the Colombian market and it is inconsistent with the standards of identity for distilled spirits sold in the United States, the European Union, Canada, and nearly every other major spirits market. Unlike Colombia's proposal, these markets base their standards of identity on the raw materials used to produce distilled spirits, not on their chemical composition. Naturally occurring constituents produced in the fermentation and distillation process, such as congeners, esters, and aldehydes, among others, are integral to the distinctive flavor characteristics of the various brands and categories of distilled spirits, and there is no scientific evidence to suggest that the presence of these constituents is the concentrations found in distilled spirits is harmful to consumers. In addition, Colombia's proposal to impose minimum and maximum alcohol content limits on distilled spirits could also adversely affect U.S. exports. For this reason, the United States has expressed significant concerns with Colombia both bilaterally in meetings of the TBT Committee.

The European Union

<u>Bilateral Engagement</u>

The United States has actively engaged the European Union (EU) on TBT-related matters in multilateral fora, including the TBT Committee, as well as bilaterally. The United States has also used the Transatlantic Economic Council (TEC) and the United States – European Union High-Level Regulatory Cooperation Forum (HLRCF) as forums to raise concerns and encourage systemic changes in the EU approach to key TBT issues.

In addition to raising concerns with the EU regarding standards-related measures as they arise, the United States and the EU have also used these fora to coordinate their regulatory approaches, which the two sides recognized in the TEC could result in greater compatibility of effective and economically beneficial regulation and promote economic integration. Further, the United States and the EU have jointly advocated to trade and regulatory officials in key emerging markets such as Brazil, China, and India the importance of maintaining open and transparent regulatory and standards development processes, as well as jointly advocating on specific market access issues on behalf of U.S. and EU exporters.

Accreditation Rules

The United States continues to have serious concerns regarding the EU's accreditation framework set out in Regulation (EC) No 765/2008. The regulation, which applies to all sectors, became effective on January 1, 2010. It requires each Member State to appoint a single national accreditation body and prohibits competition among Member States' national accreditation bodies. The regulation further specifies that national accreditation bodies shall operate as public, not-for-profit entities. This means that only a single, government entity in each Member State shall be permitted to accredit conformity assessment bodies in the EU.

The EU regulation raises serious questions as to whether the EU or its Member States will continue to recognize non-EU accreditation bodies that have been accredited under the ILAC MRA and the IAF MLA and will continue to accept conformity assessments performed by such bodies. Because the regulation gives Member States discretion regarding whether to recognize non-European accreditation bodies and whether to accept conformity assessments issued by ILAC MRA and IAF MLA accredited bodies, it is possible that Member States may refuse to recognize non-European accreditation bodies and refuse to accept conformity assessments issued by these bodies. The regulation raises market access concerns for U.S. producers, whose products may have been tested and/or certified by conformity assessment bodies accredited by non-European accreditation bodies.

The EU's approach to foreign accreditation bodies is undermined by the view of the European co-operation for Accreditation (EA). The EA has acknowledged that attestations of conformity assessment results issued by bodies that have been accredited by non-European bodies that are ILAC MRA or IAF MLA signatories are as reliable as those issued by European bodies complying with the new accreditation requirements set forth in Regulation 765.

The United States has raised its concerns over Regulation 765 with the EU in the TBT Committee. In response, the EU has stated that the regulation does not apply outside of the EU, and thus, will not affect U.S. accreditors or the international conformity assessment system. However, these assurances appear to conflict with the measure's provisions, which do not limit its application in that way.

The United States is also concerned with an apparent lack of technical basis for the assumptions behind the regulation, including that: (1) accreditation activities should be limited to governmental bodies or bodies that act in the exercise of official authority; (2) accreditations should be viewed with a higher degree of confidence when provided by a single national accreditation body; and (3) competition could compromise the quality of accreditations and should therefore be limited. In fact, the United States holds the opposite views, and the EU has failed to give an adequate explanation of the basis for its assumptions.

Similarly, the EU has not explained why the regulation imposes conditions on accreditors operating in the EU market that extend beyond the relevant ISO/IEC standard applied under the ILAC MRA and the IAF MLA.

From a broader standpoint, the United States is concerned about the implications of the EU's system for the international accreditation system under the ILAC MRA and the IAF MLA. In particular, the United States is concerned that the EU may be seeking to undermine this system by encouraging governments to adopt the EU approach. If governments do so, there could be a substantial adverse effect on U.S. exports, and the United States may be required to alter the manner in which U.S. goods are certified to meet product standards in export markets.

Thus far, the EU's ILAC signatories appear to be cooperating with non-EU ILAC signatories and confirming the equivalence of their respective accreditations if applicable requirements have been met. However, the United States continues to be concerned about the Regulation's potential impact on the recognition of non-EU accreditation bodies under the ILAC MRA and the IAF MLA and the acceptance of conformity assessments performed by ILAC MRA and IAF MLA accredited bodies. As a result, the United States is continuing to urge the EU to revisit its approach to accreditation. In the short term, the United States is also encouraging the EU to issue guidance to Member States indicating that accreditations by ILAC MRA and IAF MLA signatories are no less reliable than accreditations by European national bodies, which would allow Member States to accept testing and certification from non-EU bodies that have been accredited by an ILAC MRA or IAF MLA signatory.

<u>Borates and Nickel Compounds – Classification and Labeling Requirements</u>

Since 2007, the EU proposed changing the classification and labeling requirements for 896 substances, including borates, nickel carbonates and other nickel compounds. Under the EU's previous regime, the Dangerous Substances Directive (DSD), the EU proposed classifying these compounds under Category 2, which would have included product and packaging restrictions. For instance, Category 2 would have required products containing borates above a certain concentration to carry a "skull and crossbones" label, thus discouraging manufacturers from using borates.

In December 2008, the EU decided to replace the DSD with a new regime for classification and labeling, the Regulation on the Classification, Labelling and Packaging of Substances and Mixtures (CLP). Under the CLP, the EU would continue to classify borates and other nickel compounds in a stringent category known as Category 1B, which would subject them to product and packaging restrictions, including a requirement to use labels showing a picture of an "exploding man," along with warning and risk phrases.

The U.S. industry believes that the classification of borates under this new category is unnecessarily trade-restrictive, and is not based on "normal handling and use" of downstream products containing borates. Industry raised further concerns that the classification of borates in this manner would lead to restrictions and bans on using borates in certain products (*e.g.,* cosmetics, detergents, and fertilizers) under related EU directives.

Various industrial producers have launched cases in the UK courts and in the European Court of

First Instance seeking to annul the borates and nickel classifications. In addition, the United States has frequently raised questions regarding these issues in the TBT Committee. In particular, the United States continues to be concerned with the EU's procedures for classifying borates and certain nickel compounds, specifically regarding possible flaws in the EU's classification methodology, the procedures the EU used in transferring these classifications from the DSD to the CLP, and the effect these classifications will have under other EU measures, such as the EU's chemical regulation, REACH. In 2011, the United States will continue to monitor the potential adverse trade effects of the EU's nickel and borates classifications as well as the methodological issues mentioned above.

Chemicals – REACH Regulation

The *2010 TBT Report* recounts substantial U.S. concerns with the EU's chemical regulation, REACH. REACH impacts virtually every industrial sector, from automobiles to textiles, because it regulates chemicals as a substance, in preparations, and in products. It imposes extensive registration, testing and data requirements on tens of thousands of chemicals. REACH also subjects certain chemicals to an authorization process that would prohibit them from being placed on the EU market except as authorized for specific uses by the European Commission.

U.S. industry has expressed specific concerns with the fact that REACH requires polymer manufacturers and importers to register reacted monomers in many circumstances. This is problematic because reacted monomers no longer exist as individual substances in polymers and would not create exposure concerns in the EU. In addition, EU polymer manufacturers generally can rely on the registrations of their monomer suppliers and do not need to be individually registered. As a result, the reacted monomer registration requirement provides an incentive for distributors to stop importing polymers and switch to EU polymer suppliers. The United States has pressed the EU to eliminate the requirement to register reacted monomers in polymers entering the EU market.

Moreover, REACH contains notification and communication obligations with respect to substances on the Candidate List, a list of substances that may become subject to authorization. Differing interpretations between the Commission and several Member States regarding when these obligations apply has created uncertainty about how to comply with these obligations. The Commission has indicated that notification and communication obligations apply if a substance on the List is present in an article in concentrations above 0.1 percent of the article's entire weight; however, these Member States have stated that these obligations should apply when a substance on the List is present in concentrations above 0.1 percent of the weight of the article's components or homogenous parts. In 2010, these Member States pushed the Commission to reverse its position as a way of protecting the EU market from imports since a reinterpretation would impact imports. A change in interpretation would present a much more difficult compliance problem for U.S. industry since it would require companies to perform an analysis of individual component concentration levels in their products, which would be extremely time-consuming and burdensome. Given that an alteration of the EU's approach could substantially disrupt U.S. exports, the United States has asked the EU to ensure that all Member States follow the Commission's current interpretation.

Other problematic issues with the EU's REACH regime include inadequate transparency, differing registration requirements for EU and non-EU entities, and substantial data requirements.

The United States has raised concerns regarding REACH at every TBT Committee meeting since 2003, and has been joined by many other delegations, including Argentina, Australia, Brazil, Canada, Chile, China, Colombia, Cuba, the Dominican Republic, Ecuador, Egypt, El Salvador, India, Israel, Japan, Korea, Malaysia, Mexico, Qatar, Russia, Singapore, Switzerland, Taiwan, and Thailand. The United States also has raised its concerns regarding REACH directly with the EU and has worked with the European Chemicals Agency on specific technical issues. The United States will continue to monitor closely REACH implementation in 2011, and will raise trade concerns, as appropriate, in the TBT Committee and other pertinent fora. A potential new venue for pursuing these concerns is the U.S. – EU Chemicals Dialogue agreed to at the December 2010 TEC meeting.

Industrial Products – Country of Origin Labeling for Imports Only

The EU is considering adopting country of origin labeling requirements for leather, travel goods, hand bags, apparel, textiles and textile articles, ceramics, glassware, jewelry, furniture, bedding, lamps and lighting, brooms and brushes, screws, nuts, bolts, tools, and tires. The EU Parliament approved these requirements in October 2010, and they are pending in the European Council. While the United States supports country of origin labeling requirements adopted to provide consumers with information about the products they buy, the United States is concerned that the EU's requirements would only apply to imported products. As a result, the United States raised this issue with the EU at the November 2010 TBT Committee meeting.

Hazardous Substance Restrictions

The EU's Directive on the Restriction of the Use of Certain Hazardous Substances in Electrical and Electronic Equipment (RoHS) prohibits placing certain categories of electrical and electronic equipment on the EU market that contain chemicals such as lead, mercury, cadmium, and hexavalent chromium. The RoHS directive includes certain application-specific exemptions from the prohibitions. The EU considers requests for additional exemptions on an ongoing basis.

The United States supports the EU's objectives of protecting human health and the environment; however, the United States is concerned about the transparency and predictability of the EU's process and timing for considering exemption requests and the absence of a common approach to enforcement in all EU Member States. As noted in last year's report, the EU was expected to revise its RoHS directive in late 2010 or early 2011. The EU has not yet adopted revisions, and it is unclear when this process will move forward. The United States continues to urge the EU to provide an adequate opportunity for U.S. stakeholders to provide input into the revision process.

On substance, the United States is urging the EU to adopt a revision that clarifies the relationship between REACH and RoHS and includes an improved exemption process that takes into account the products concerned when determining the length of time for which exemptions apply. The United States has also urged the EU to ensure that any decision to expand the RoHS directive's scope of covered products be informed by a thorough impact assessment, and that any decisions regarding additional restrictions included in a revised directive are based on science, taking into account intended end uses and all available scientific and technical information. These revisions would help ensure transparency and legal certainty regarding how products will be treated.

Ride-on Lawnmowers – Unique French Requirements

The United States continues to have concerns with respect to the French Ministry of Agriculture's (MoA) "skirt" requirement for ride-on lawnmowers, a measure that France neither published as part of an official law or decree nor notified to the WTO. The MoA requirement for ride-on lawnmowers already has disrupted U.S. lawnmower exports to France. If other Member States were to adopt this requirement, a significant portion of the approximately $1 billion in annual U.S. shipments of lawnmowers to Europe could be adversely affected.

The United States is not aware of any technical basis for requiring ride-on lawnmowers to be fitted with an extra piece of equipment (or "skirt"). U.S. officials understand that the skirt requirement represents a unique French requirement that is neither consistent with requirements in other EU Member States, nor based on internationally developed ASTM or ISO ride-on lawnmower standards used throughout the world. Accordingly, the United States has requested that the Commission share accident data it believes supports the French position that installation of the lawnmower skirt would increase bystander safety, and any analysis undertaken by the MoA on the potential fire hazard that installation of the skirt could create. The United States clarified that if this information does not exist or does not support the necessity of the skirt requirement, the Commission should recommend that France base its ride-on lawnmower requirements on a relevant international standard or eliminate the skirt requirement altogether. Both EU and U.S. lawnmower manufacturers have challenged the French lawnmower requirement as well.

During 2010, the MoA worked on a revision to the EN 836 standard to address these concerns. In October 2010, a working group advising MoA on the revision concluded that total enclosure of all transmission moving parts was unnecessary, directly rejecting the MoA's position that complete coverage is required. The working group also acknowledged that the risk of fire from total enclosure is significant, and that attention in the revision process should be shifted to the pinch points only, instead of concentrating on all transmission moving parts.

While the position developed by the working group is acceptable to U.S. and European industry, the MoA does not appear to be wavering on its position that complete coverage is necessary. As a result, producers must either comply with MoA's skirt requirement for sales in the French market or face recalls. In addition, U.S. companies have complained of being singled out for enforcement action by French customs officials.

The United States will continue to press the EU to address this issue in 2011.

Wine – Labeling Requirements

As described in last year's report, the EU continues to seek exclusive use of so-called "traditional terms" such as tawny, ruby, reserve, classic, and chateau on wine labels, but may allow third country producers to use such terms pursuant to an agreement with the EU or contingent on the regulation of those terms in their home market. Under the United States – EU wine agreement, the EU permitted the use of certain terms on U.S. wines sold in the EU for a three-year extendable period, but then declined to extend the period past March 2009. As part of its effort to redesign its

Common Market Organization on wine, the EU published its new regulation (EC No 607/2009) on July 14, 2009, laying down detailed rules for implementation of EC regulation 479/2008 with regard to protected designations of origin and geographical indication, traditional terms, labeling, and presentation of certain wine products. The regulation leaves enforcement to EU Member States. It is unclear how Member States will enforce the regulation or how the Commission plans to ensure consistency of interpretation across Member States.

The United States continues to have serious concerns regarding these measures, which severely restrict the ability of non-EU wine producers to use common or descriptive and commercially valuable terms to describe their products, on the grounds that those terms are traditionally associated with European wines. The United States is also concerned about continued EU efforts to expand the list of so-called "traditional terms" to include additional commercially valuable terms. Some of these terms do not have a common definition across all EU Member States, and the United States is not aware of any effort to monitor or limit the use of those terms within the EU. Additionally, the United States remains concerned about the EU's decision to withdraw permission to use certain "traditional terms" under the U.S. – EU wine agreement, as well as the EU's limitation on the use of traditional expressions in trademarks.

While the EU attempts to justify limitations on the use of traditional terms by indicating that they could be used to mislead consumers, these terms have been used without incident on U.S. wines in the EU market for many years, which suggests that there is no such risk. During 2011, the United States will continue to coordinate with the U.S. wine exporters on how best to address and resolve concerns regarding the EU's wine policy.

India

Bilateral Engagement

The United States discusses TBT matters with India during TBT Committee meetings and on the margins of these meetings. U.S. government officials also discuss such matters with Indian officials under the U.S. – India Trade Policy Forum (TPF), the TPF's Tariff and Non-tariff Barriers and Agriculture Focus Groups, the U.S. – India Commercial Dialogue and the High-Technology Cooperation Group.

In addition, the U.S. Trade and Development Agency (USTDA) is also funding a program with the Confederation of Indian Industry (CII) to facilitate India's development of a transparent and more streamlined system of standards, conformity assessment, and technical regulations. CII and ANSI have added India-specific content to ANSI's standards portal (www.standardsportal.org). CII and ANSI also held workshops on standards for safe storage of liquefied natural gas and aerospace standards in February 2010, and held an exchange on biometrics standards under this initiative in July 2010.

Cosmetics – Registration Requirements

U.S. industry has raised concerns regarding India's proposed "Drugs and Cosmetics (Amendment) Rules, 2007." In particular, the U.S. industry expressed concerns about initial aspects of India's proposal, including a proposed registration system that only appeared to be targeted at imports. U.S. industry was concerned that these requirements would create an unreasonably costly and burdensome registration system and would result in unnecessary delays for cosmetic products being brought to market.

The United States shared industry's concerns and requested India to notify the measure to the WTO, to delay enforcement to allow a reasonable time for Members to comment, and to afford suppliers a reasonable period to comply with the new requirements. India eventually notified the measure, and the United States submitted comments including concerns raised by U.S. stakeholders through India's TBT Inquiry Point.

In response to U.S. comments, India's Ministry of Health (MoH) made a number of clarifications and modifications to the proposed measure in 2009 and, in July 2010, issued Guidelines on Import and Registration of Cosmetics. These guidelines provide additional clarity, such as clarifying the definition of "brand"; allowing manufacturing sites of a parent company to be registered under a single registration; applying a single registration fee to all product lines of the same brand; and providing for fast track review of products currently on the market. U.S. industry continues to express concerns regarding whether there will be an adequate compliance period and whether stickering will be allowed for country-specific information, among other issues. The United States will continue to raise these issues with India in 2011.

Food and Distilled Spirits – Nutritional Labeling

The United States is concerned by nutritional labeling requirements that India adopted in 2009. In particular, the United States is concerned that India's measure requires labels of distilled spirits to provide the date of production, which is irrelevant in the case of distilled spirits since such products have an indefinite shelf life. The United States is also concerned with further requirements addressing: (1) the labeling of proprietary foods; (2) the declaration and calculation of certain nutrient values; (3) the criteria for labeling a product as "trans fat free"; (4) the allowance of stickering on products; and (5) the rules for front of pack flavoring declarations using the statement "CONTAINS ADDED FLAVOUR."

The United States has repeatedly expressed concerns about this issue directly to India in writing and at the margins of TBT Committee meetings. India has not been responsive to U.S. concerns. Most recently, in February 2010, the U.S. government submitted further comments to India on its outstanding concerns, but India has not addressed these concerns. The United States will continue to press India to resolve this issue in 2011.

Telecommunications Equipment – Information Security Regulations

U.S. industry has raised significant concerns with a number of telecommunications equipment requirements that India's Department of Telecommunications has adopted, including licensing amendments adopted in December 2009 and March 2010, and a "template agreement for security and business continuity" adopted in July 2010. These requirements would be a mandatory part of private commercial contracts between foreign telecommunications service providers and vendors of foreign telecommunications-related equipment, products, and services in India. However, they would not apply to telecom equipment and products manufactured in India. Under these measures, any vendor seeking to sell foreign manufactured telecom equipment and products to Indian telecom service providers would be required to: (1) deposit their source codes in escrow;

(2) transfer their technology to Indian companies; and (3) follow burdensome testing and certification requirements. The U.S. and global telecom equipment industries have indicated these requirements could halt billions of dollars of equipment sales in India.

U.S. government officials have raised this issue with India in many different fora and at many different levels of government, including in the TBT Committee and during the September 2010 U.S.-India Trade Policy Forum. U.S. officials also raised this issue with officials of India's Office of the Prime Minister before President Obama's visit to India in November 2010.

In response to U.S. comments, India suspended its implementation of the "template agreement" and agreed to review its security requirements. In January 2011, the Ministry of Communications and Information Technology announced a 100-day action plan to develop a new security regime for telecom equipment. At this time, it appears that India is planning to base its regime on the problematic template agreement. Further, India has not yet announced a transparent process for developing this new regime. The United States continues to urge India to provide a draft of any revised regulations so that interested parties have an opportunity to provide comments.

Indonesia

Bilateral Engagement

The United States discusses TBT matters with Indonesia both bilaterally and during meetings of the TBT Committee. The United States – Indonesia TIFA Council provides a forum for bilateral discussions on a variety of trade-related issues, including standards-related issues. Indonesia also participates actively on standards and conformance issues in APEC.

Bahasa Labeling Requirement

In September 2010, Indonesia announced that it will require all imported products to bear original labels in the Bahasa language and will require these labels to be affixed to processed food products before they are shipped to Indonesia. Previously, Indonesia had permitted importers in Indonesia to apply sticker labels with Bahasa translations once imported products cleared customs. This new policy will significantly raise compliance costs for U.S. industry and could completely shut off U.S. processed product exports to Indonesia, resulting in a market loss of up to $220 million on an annual basis.

The United States raised this issue with Indonesia during the TBT Committee meeting in November 2010. U.S. officials noted that Indonesia has not clearly explained the new labeling rule to its trading partners nor notified it to the WTO.

The United States and Indonesia held a series of meetings in February 2011 to try to resolve this issue. During these meetings, Indonesian officials indicated that producers could comply with the new Bahasa language requirements by applying supplementary labels, but refused to clarify whether "stickers" would be considered adequate for this purpose. Indonesian officials also did not clarify whether the supplementary labels could be affixed at the port of entry after products clear customs.

The United States will continue to urge Indonesia to clarify outstanding issues arising from its new labeling measure and to consider suspending its implementation in order to notify the measure to the WTO and take comments into account from interested parties.

<u>Food, Supplements, Drugs, and Cosmetics – Distribution License Requirements</u>

In August 2009, Indonesia issued proposed requirements governing the distribution of food, food supplements, drugs, and cosmetics. The proposed requirements prohibited the distribution of food, food supplements, drugs, and cosmetics in Indonesia without first obtaining a distribution license. The criteria for receiving a license differed by product type and were based on several factors, including whether certain ingredients are halal.

For example, under these proposed requirements, any pharmaceutical products or drugs containing certain animal substances would not qualify for a distribution license in the absence of an "emergency," and all such products would be required to bear a label indicating "Swine Content." Further, drug products manufactured using substances sourced from swine in the production process would be required to bear a label indicating that: "The manufacturing process involves a substance that [is] sourced from swine and has been purified so that [it is] not detected on final product." Food sourced from swine would be subject to a separate set of emergency procedures. Distribution licenses also could not be awarded for products containing alcohol, such as certain pharmaceuticals, cosmetics, and food flavorings.

Indonesia's proposed requirements threatened to disrupt U.S. exports to Indonesia of foods (many flavorings contain alcohol, sometimes in *de minimis* amounts); drugs (many products, such as cough syrups and other over-the-counter drugs, contain alcohol and others, such as gelatin capsules and vaccines, are sourced from swine); and cosmetics (many products contain alcohol). The United States was particularly concerned that the requirements could have disrupted trade in critical medicines, such as vaccines, as well as trade in many other products.

The United States raised concerns about Indonesia's proposed requirements in the TBT Committee in 2009 and 2010. The United States explained that while it respected Indonesia's right to regulate halal products, Indonesia should have developed and proposed to apply its requirements affecting trade in halal products in a transparent manner and should have made additional efforts to ensure that the measures would not disrupt trade. In addition, the United States conveyed its concern that many of the operational details of the licensing system were unclear. The United States requested Indonesia to suspend enforcement of the measure until it notifies it to the WTO and takes comments from trading partners into account.

As a result of U.S. efforts, Indonesia agreed to revoke the measure. During the November 2010 meeting of the TBT Committee, Indonesia confirmed that the measure had been revoked.

<u>Meat and Poultry – Halal Certification</u>

Indonesia only allows the sale of meat and poultry products that have been certified halal by certifiers recognized by Indonesia's Council of Ulama ("MUI"). Halal certification involves certifying that the product has been slaughtered and handled in a manner consistent with Islamic law.

On March 9, 2009 MUI issued a decree announcing that a new list of MUI recognized halal certifiers would become effective October 1, 2009, superseding all previous MUI recognized halal certifiers. MUI did not make publicly available or notify to the WTO the new procedures and criteria for recognition and inclusion of certifiers on the new list.

MUI published the new list of halal certifiers on October 22, 2009, 21 days after the decree's effective date, causing a 22 day disruption in all halal trade to Indonesia. The new halal certifier list did not include any halal certifiers for halal trade in poultry or lamb. The list also excluded several U.S. processed food halal certifiers that MUI has historically recognized.

U.S. officials repeatedly registered concerns regarding MUI's certifier list during TBT Committee meetings in 2009 and 2010. Among other issues, U.S. officials noted that the process to apply for and gain MUI approval was not set out in the March 2009 decree and was not made available to the public. As a result, many certifiers did not know whether they were required to re-apply for approval and were not aware of the new rules for halal accreditation.

In response to U.S. concerns, Indonesia's TBT Inquiry Point issued a communication in May 2010 claiming that Indonesia would accept e-mail applications from U.S. poultry and lamb producers for halal certifications sent to MUI. During bilateral discussions on the margins of the November 2010 TBT Committee meeting, Indonesian officials clarified that MUI lacks confidence in the U.S. slaughtering process for poultry and lamb and that it would not approve any applications from the United States until it conducted an audit of the U.S. halal slaughtering system for both poultry and lamb. MUI officials visited several U.S. facilities in December 2010 and accredited four U.S. poultry certifiers in early 2011, restoring U.S. access to Indonesia's market for halal poultry.

While this is a welcome development, U.S. officials will continue to work with Indonesia to secure market access for all U.S. industries seeking to export halal products to Indonesia.

Japan

Bilateral Engagement

The United States discusses TBT matters with Japan during and on the margins of WTO TBT Committee meetings. The United States will continue to raise potential TBT issues with Japan in bilateral fora, including the U.S. – Japan Economic Harmonization Initiative. This initiative was launched in November 2010 and aims to promote harmonization of approaches that facilitate trade, address business climate and specific trade issues, and advance coordination on issues of common interest. The United States intends to raise standards-related issues arising in such areas as agriculture, medical devices and pharmaceuticals, cosmetics, nutritional supplements, and information and communication technologies.

In the area of pharmaceuticals and medical devices, for example, Japan is setting clearer performance measures than in the past for reviewers involved in approving new products. There are remaining issues, however, with the lag in the availability of new drugs and devices in Japan compared to their availability in other advanced nations which need to be addressed. For nutritional supplements, the United States has urged Japan to adopt a system allowing ingredient-specific health claims that is science-based and transparent as well as to instill greater transparency in the operations of Japan's quarantine stations in order to streamline import procedures. The United States also continues to raise the need for greater clarification of Japan's classification criteria for drugs, foods, and food additives and the process it uses to categorize new ingredients. In the areas of cosmetics and "quasi-drugs," the United States continues to encourage Japan to make improvements in its regulatory environment, including for labeling and claims, its importation procedures, and overall transparency.

The United States is also encouraging Japan to enhance the overall transparency of its regulatory regime and to improve its public comment procedures.

Organic Product Requirements

U.S. organics exports to Japan are limited by Japan's ban on alkali extracted humic acid, a substance that USDA permits for use on U.S. organic crops. While Japan has permitted some forms of this substance to be used, it still bans most forms of the acid. The United States has focused its efforts on persuading Japan to allow the use of lignin sulfonate as a flotation device for cleaning fresh fruits in the organic production process, but Japan continues to request additional information from the United States regarding this subject.

In addition, Japan's zero tolerance policy for pesticide and herbicide residues on organic products continues to be problematic for U.S. industry. Even though these substances are not applied to organic crops, they are often present in the natural environment, which makes achieving zero residue level very difficult. In addition, Japan's zero tolerance policy appears to exceed the Codex Guidelines for the Production, Processing, Labeling and Marketing of Organically Produced Foods. These guidelines apply to the process by which organic foods are produced, and do not mandate specific maximum residue levels for pesticides and contaminants.

Largely, in response in response to U.S. engagement on this issue, Japan's Ministry of Agriculture, Forestry, and Fisheries (MAFF) announced in April 2009 that it would begin revising Japan's requirements for organic plants, organic processed foods, organic livestock products and organic feeds. In 2010, MAFF established study committees comprising growers, retailers, consumers and academics to review different aspects of Japan's regulations. While MAFF indicated that during the review process it would revisit its zero tolerance requirement with stakeholders, there have been no such discussions thus far. MAFF is scheduled to complete its review process by the end of 2011.

The United States will continue to monitor the situation closely in 2011 and press Japan to modify its requirements in a manner that will improve access to Japan's market for U.S. organic products.

Korea

Bilateral Engagement

Korea and the United States hold regularly scheduled bilateral consultations to address potential bilateral trade issues, including technical barriers, as they emerge. These bilateral consultations, led by USTR with participation from the full range of relevant U.S. agencies, serve as an important forum for discussing and resolving these issues and are augmented by a broad range of senior-level policy discussions. In 2010, bilateral trade consultations were held in May and September, leading to the resolution of a number of TBT issues. A similar slate of meetings will be held in 2011. In addition, USTR and other agency officials meet with their counterparts in the Korean government on a regular basis to discuss trade-related issues, for example, in the context of meetings of the TBT Committee.

Conformity Assessment

The pending U.S.-Korea Free Trade Agreement (KORUS) would address conformity assessment issues in several ways, most notably by committing Korea to provide national treatment in its recognition of conformity assessment bodies, to recognize conformity assessment bodies on the basis of published criteria, and to take steps to implement Phase II of the APEC Telecomm MRA with respect to the United States as soon as possible. At the current time, however, Korean laws and regulations generally limit the bodies that may test and certify products for compliance with Korean electrical safety requirements to "domestic nonprofit organizations equipped with suitable testing equipment and qualified testing personnel..." U.S. industry is concerned that the inability of U.S. testing and certification bodies to test and certify products for the Korean market disadvantages U.S. manufacturers on account of the fact that U.S. manufacturers must have their products tested and certified in Korea, which can be inconvenient, time consuming, and costly and cause delays to market.

There were positive developments on this issue in 2009 and 2010 with respect to safety testing for lithium ion batteries and energy efficiency testing for refrigerators. In 2009, following active engagement by the United States, Korea agreed to allow non-Korean conformity assessment bodies to test for conformity with new Korean safety regulations for lithium-ion batteries. In May 2010, Korea issued revised regulations governing energy efficiency testing for refrigerators to reflect longstanding U.S. concerns. Under the revised regulations, Korea will accept energy efficiency data from non-Korean testing bodies, both to determine whether a product meets Korea's minimum energy efficiency standards for placing a product on Korea's market and as part of a challenge process under which firms can question a competitor's energy efficiency test results. U.S. officials are urging Korea to adopt approaches similar to those it has applied with respect to batteries and refrigerators to other such products for which test results are required.

Motor Vehicles – Proposed Fuel Efficiency and Emissions Requirements

Since July 2009, Korea has been in the process of drafting regulations that would establish new fuel efficiency and green house gas emission requirements for automobiles. While the United States shares Korea's interest in promoting fuel efficiency and reducing green house gas emissions, U.S. officials sought to ensure that the regulations were designed and drafted in a way that would not undermine market access for U.S. autos, while meeting Korea's environmental objectives.

In December 2010, Korea agreed to include in its final regulation a provision that allows manufacturers that sold 4,500 or fewer automobiles in Korea in 2009 (the regulation's base year) to comply with the regulation from 2012-2015 if the fleet they sell in Korea comes within 19 percent of the new Korean requirements. In other words, the Korean fleet of qualifying automakers can comply with the regulation even if their fleet average fuel economy is 19 percent lower than would normally be required. This will help level the playing field for U.S. autos in the Korean market.

Organic products – Requirements and Conformity Assessment Issues

In June 2008, Korea published its new Processed Organic Foods Regulation, with a proposed implementation date of January 1, 2010. The regulation would have required all products claiming to be organic to be certified as organic by a certification body accredited by Korea's Ministry of Food, Agriculture, Forestry and Fisheries (MIFAFF). Many U.S. producers and certifiers have been reluctant to attempt to seek certification and accreditation under the new regulation, in part due to Korea's zero-tolerance policy on biotechnology presence in organic products as well as due to the increased costs that compliance with the regulation would impose. Further, because the Korean regulation does not provide for Korea to negotiate agreements for equivalency or recognition of foreign organics programs, implementation of the regulation could have significantly impeded, or even halted, U.S. organics exports to Korea.

In response to concerns raised by the United States and other exporting countries, in August 2010 MIFAFF agreed to allow foreign organic products to be sold in Korea until December 31, 2012 without having to be certified by a MIFAFF-accredited certifier. In the meantime, MIFAFF is revising and consolidating its organics regulations, which are expected to include a provision that will allow equivalency negotiations between the United States and Korea to proceed.

The United States will continue to urge Korea to re-consider its zero-tolerance policy for biotechnology presence in organics.

Processed Food Products – Mandatory Biotechnology Labeling

In October 2008, the Korean Food and Drug Administration proposed expanding its mandatory biotechnology labeling for food products containing bioengineered ingredients to include processed products such as vegetable oils and distilled spirits. Under this proposal, certain processed products with ingredients derived from biotechnology commodities, such as corn and soybeans, would require a label indicating that they are derived from biotechnology products.

The United States has concerns with the negative effect on trade that results from the potentially misleading nature of mandatory labeling of food products containing or derived from biotechnology. By expanding the scope of products covered by its mandatory labeling regime to include products such as distilled spirits, Korea's proposal would result in an even greater disruption of trade. U.S. officials have continued to urge Korea to reconsider the need for expanding the regime. A decision from Korea on whether to adopt the proposed requirement remains pending.

Solar Panels – Design Requirements

In 2010, U.S. officials continued to raise concerns that certain types of thin-film solar panels (TFSP) manufactured by U.S. industry cannot be placed on the Korean market. Since July 2008, Korea has required solar panels to be certified by the Korea Management Energy Corporation (KEMCO) in order to be sold in Korea. KEMCO will only certify solar panels as safe if they meet the mandatory Korean standard for TFSP (KS61646:2007 Thin film terrestrial photovoltaic

(PV) modules – Design qualification and type approval). This standard incorporates much of IEC 61646 (Thin-film terrestrial photovoltaic (PV) modules – Design qualification and type approval), but its application is limited to amorphous silicon (A-Si) type thin film solar panels whereas the IEC standard applies to all types of thin film solar panels. Korea has not adopted a standard for other types of TFSP.

As a result, other leading types of panels, including Cadmium Telluride (CdTe) and Copper Indium (di) Selenide (CIS), cannot be tested or certified under the Korean standard and accordingly cannot gain the necessary certification to be placed on the Korean market. Korea's lack of an applicable standard for other types of TFSP will also affect panels made with Gallium arsenide (GaAs), which is emerging as a commercially proven technology. According to U.S. industry, Korea is the only country in the world that specifically restricts application of the IEC standard to only one of the three leading types of thin film panels.

Korea has explained that it adopted its standard based on concerns about the presence of cadmium in other types of solar panels or the use of cadmium in the production process. In bilateral discussions and in meetings of the TBT Committee, Korea has indicated that it is conducting a study to determine whether it might be feasible to include other types of TFSPs within the scope of its solar panel standard. It has stated that the study should be completed in 2011.

The United States recognizes the environmental dangers of cadmium and, like Korea, maintains legal requirements on safe use of cadmium. However, the residual level of cadmium in other types of solar panels, currently sold in the United States and other markets, is minimal. The United States is not aware of any scientific or technical evidence indicating that there are risks from using thin film solar panels that are not covered by the Korean version of the IEC standard. Thus, the United States continues to urge Korea to adopt the IEC 61646 standard without limiting its application to A-Si thin-film solar panels.

Malaysia

Bilateral Engagement

The United States discusses TBT matters with Malaysia during TBT Committee meetings, bilaterally on the margins of those meetings, and during TPP negotiations. Malaysia also participates actively on standards and conformance issues in APEC.

Meat and Poultry Products – Halal Standards

In December 2009, Malaysia published a final standard for halal food production. The standard requires meat packing facilities to be dedicated exclusively to halal production. The requirement exceeds the terms of the Codex halal standard, which allows producers to use dedicated lines for halal meat products within a facility that includes non-halal production. Malaysian officials have cited a lack of trust in the purity and reliability of halal meat production chains outside Malaysia as the basis for the new requirement, but Malaysia has presented no evidence to support this view, despite repeated U.S. requests.

U.S. producers have indicated that they are willing to produce to importing countries' halal standards when those standards are reasonable and do not require an entirely segregated supply chain. U.S. industry estimates that U.S. exports to Malaysia of halal beef and poultry could grow dramatically if Malaysia adopts reasonable and reliable halal production standards and import licensing practices.

Malaysia has committed that its new halal requirements will take effect for U.S. producers only after Malaysia audits U.S. meat production facilities. Malaysia has requested to carry out several audits, but U.S. officials have requested further clarity on audit parameters before facilitating this request.

Malaysia has failed to notify its halal standard to the WTO as a technical regulation, claiming that the halal standard is voluntary and does not need to be notified. However, Malaysia currently bans imports of non-halal meat, a practice that Malaysian officials have explained as useful for avoiding consumer confusion since non-halal meat products may not be sold in Malaysia. Contrary to this explanation from Malaysian officials, the United States has confirmed that non-halal products are widely available for sale in segregated portions of Malaysian food stores. Thus, it does not appear that Malaysia bans all non-halal products, but only non-halal imports. The United States will continue to raise this issue with Malaysia in 2011.

Mexico

Bilateral Engagement

The United States discusses TBT matters with Mexico during TBT Committee meetings and on the margins of these meetings. The United States also discusses specific trade concerns and systemic issues with Mexico in the context of the NAFTA and subordinate trade working groups (TWGs) established to address particular standards-related issues. Canada participates in these sessions as well. As one example, the NAFTA TWG that addresses food labeling and packaging helped increase cooperation among the NAFTA parties regarding food laboratories and nutritional labeling. The United States and Mexico also engage on standards and regulatory issues as part of the U.S. – Mexico High-Level Regulatory Cooperation Council, which was established in 2010.

Conformity Assessment Procedures

Under Article 908.2 of the NAFTA, Mexico is required to accredit, approve, license, or otherwise recognize conformity assessment bodies (*e.g.,* certification bodies or testing laboratories) in the United States on terms no less favorable than those applied to conformity assessment bodies in Mexico. While applications by U.S. conformity assessment bodies that test electrical and electronic goods for accreditation had previously been delayed, these applications were finally approved in 2007 and 2008.

Despite this positive development, the United States continued to ask Mexico for further clarification of its accreditation procedures to ensure that Mexico will continue to provide non-discriminatory treatment for all conformity assessment bodies, including those located in the United States. In particular, the United States urged Mexico to clarify whether an application for a new accreditation or an expansion of an existing accreditation can be submitted at any time or only in response to a specific call to certifiers. The United States also urged Mexico to set a reasonable period for evaluating accreditation requests so that U.S. conformity assessment bodies can avoid long delays in the accreditation process.

Significant progress was made on this issue in 2010. In August, Mexico announced that it would recognize testing and certification results from certain conformity assessment bodies in the United States (as well as Canada). In particular, Mexico indicated that testing and conformity assessments conducted in the United States that indicate that certain electronic products comply with U.S. requirements would be sufficient to demonstrate conformity with Mexican requirements. As a result, U.S. suppliers will no longer need to re-test and re-certify their products to Mexican requirements to ship them to Mexico. According to industry, this change will save companies that manufacture these products, on average, several hundred thousand dollars or more annually in compliance costs.

Certain Mexican conformity assessment bodies have challenged this determination in court, which has prevented some U.S. suppliers from taking advantage of Mexico's willingness to accept test results from U.S. conformity assessment bodies. However, the United States has received no reports that have chosen to satisfy Mexico's product requirements by choosing to have their products tested in the United States have encountered problems in exporting those goods to Mexico.

In 2010, Mexico also announced new rules that would streamline conformity assessment procedures for shipments of medical devices and certain over-the-counter (OTC) drugs from the United States. Under these rules, any producer or importer of medical devices or equipment can obtain a sanitary registration within 35 days, provided that U.S. regulators have approved the product for sale. This agreement reportedly has also been the subject of a legal challenge by Mexican producers.

Mexico's steps in this area are welcome and the United States will continue to monitor this area in 2011 to ensure that U.S. companies can take full advantage of the new opportunities Mexico has provided.

Food Products – Nutritional Labeling

In 2009, Mexico proposed to amend its nutritional labeling requirements, notifying to the WTO for comment the *"Draft Mexican Official Standard PROY-NOM-051-SCFI/SSA 1-2009: General Specifications for the Labeling of Pre-packaged Food and Non-alcoholic Beverages - Commercial and Health Information"* (NOM-051). Mexico asserted that the purpose of these proposed requirements was to provide consumers with greater information.

The United States submitted comments to Mexico on the proposal that posed technical questions and expressed concerns about the possible trade implications of the proposed measure. In particular, the United States expressed concerns about the impact that the labeling requirements could have on small packages and low volume producers, who were not originally exempt from the law, as well as about a lack of clear guidance on how Mexico would implement the labeling requirements. The United States also expressed concern that the measure would require a compliance certificate for all imported products, which could halt exports of processed food products.

Significant progress was made on this issue in 2010. First, the United States and Mexico engaged in a dialogue that clarified many of the issues regarding the proposed labeling measure, including: (1) Mexico's proposed requirements for disclosures regarding irradiated foods, compound ingredients and quantitative ingredients; (2) the scientific basis for Mexico's Recommended Daily Allowance (RDA) values, including how Mexico took Codex RDA values into account; (3) the basis for Mexico's energy calculations; and (4) the use of voluntary claims such as "natural," "halal," and "organic". Second, Mexico delayed implementation of the labeling rules from June 2010 to January 1, 2011, providing U.S. industry with additional time to comply. Third, in October 2010, Mexico issued a communication alleviating the U.S. concerns regarding the requirement to provide a compliance certificate. Finally, Mexico also agreed to include an exemption for imports shipped in small packages.

The United States is pleased with Mexico's willingness to modify its requirements to address U.S. concerns. In 2011, the United States will continue to monitor the implementation of Mexico's labeling requirements to ensure that they do not have an adverse effect on U.S. exports.

Telecommunications Equipment – Acceptance of U.S. Test Results

When the United States and Mexico signed the NAFTA, Mexico committed to adopt provisions necessary to accept test results from test laboratories in the United States as part of its conformity assessment procedures for telecommunications equipment. Until recently, Mexico had not moved forward to carry out its commitment, which could be implemented by concluding a MRA with the United States. Mexico's failure to do so prevented U.S. laboratories from testing telecommunications equipment for the Mexican market, and imposed additional costs on U.S. producers who were forced to send their products to Mexico for testing.

At the January, 2011 NAFTA Free Trade Commission meeting, the United States and Mexico committed to enter into a bilateral telecom MRA. During the meeting, Ambassador Kirk and Mexican Secretary of Economy Fernando Ruiz Mateos initialed a reference document laying out the basic terms of such an agreement and established a goal of signing the MRA by May 2011. The United States is currently working with Mexico to draft the MRA.

Russia

Bilateral Engagement

The United States engages with Russia regarding its technical regulations, standards, and conformity assessment procedures both on a bilateral basis and in the context of negotiations on Russia's accession to the WTO. (Once Russia joins the WTO it will be required to adhere to the TBT Agreement.) In addition, the Working Group on Business Development and Economic Relations established under the U.S. – Russia Bilateral Presidential Commission provides a forum for the United States and Russia to discuss, among other matters, standards-related regulatory cooperation.

Alcoholic Beverages – Tax Strip Stamp Requirement

In February 2010, Russia amended its laws to make all domestic alcohol producers and importers subject to the same requirements for labeling alcoholic beverages. As a result, Russia's United Federal Automated Information System now requires importers and domestic manufacturers of alcoholic beverages to print Universal Product Code data on small paper excise stamps attached to each bottle. The stamps must be sequentially-numbered, and importers and suppliers must prepare a consolidated document at the end of the year for all the strip stamp numbers. Further, suppliers and importers must report these stamps through an automated system for purposes of taxation and a manual system for customs purposes.

Russia's amended law represents a significant improvement over its previous system, which accorded different treatment for imported and domestic products. U.S. industry has indicated that the new reporting requirements are burdensome, however, and have disrupted U.S. exports to Russia. U.S. government reports also indicate that Russia's new system is expensive, difficult to use and, thus far, has been unsuccessful in meeting its goal of tracking alcohol from manufacture or importation to the retail sales point. In 2011, the United States will urge Russia to revise the stamp requirements to address these concerns.

<u>Alcoholic Beverages – Warehousing Requirements</u>

In October 2010, Russia's Federal Service for Alcohol Market Regulation (FSR) adopted regulations governing the storage of alcoholic beverages. The United States is concerned that these regulations impose onerous and unfounded restrictions on this practice. For example, the regulations prohibit storing different types of alcohol on one pallet; require that alcohol products be stored at least 15 cm from the floor; and preclude other goods from being stored with alcohol products. It is unclear what objective these requirements are intended fulfill. Further, they unnecessarily restrict access to the Russian market for U.S. alcoholic beverage exporters. In 2011, the United States will urge the FSR either to modify or abandon its new regulations.

Saudi Arabia

<u>Bilateral Engagement</u>

The United States engages with Saudi Arabia on TBT issues through the Trade and Investment Framework Agreement and at the TBT Committee.

<u>Conformity Assessment Procedures – Lack of Transparency</u>

In 2006, Saudi Arabia introduced a Certificate of Conformity (CoC) Program. With certain exceptions, this program requires every shipment of products sold in Saudi Arabia to be accompanied by a document certifying that the product conforms to the relevant Saudi technical regulation ("conformity certificate").

U.S. exporters have had difficulty complying with this requirement because Saudi Arabia has not provided detailed public guidance in English on how to do so, despite Saudi Arabia's commitment at the time it acceded to the WTO to provide such guidance. For example, it is not clear whether U.S. conformity assessment bodies may perform testing or certification that satisfied Saudi requirements or whether U.S. exporters must work with Intertek, a company with which Saudi authorities had originally contracted to provide services under the country's the now abolished International Conformity Certification Program. Intertek currently claims through its internet website to operate Saudi Arabia's product assessment program.

The United States has raised this issue with Saudi Arabia both bilaterally and in meetings of the TBT Committee since 2006. In particular, the United States has raised concerns that Saudi Arabia has still not issued guidance in English on how to comply with its CoC requirements or dissolved Intertek's web site. The United States has also urged Saudi Arabia to publish guidance on how to comply with the CoC, including the criteria that Saudi Arabia uses to recognize bodies to test and certify products for the Saudi market, and a list of conformity assessment bodies that are approved to provide testing and certification for the Saudi market.

U.S. officials discussed this issue most recently with officials of the Saudi Arabia Standards Organization (SASO) in late 2010. SASO officials clarified that SASO enters into government-to-government MRAs and government-to-private body MRAs to recognize conformity assessment bodies. Before entering into an MRA with Saudi Arabia, the United States has requested that Saudi Arabia establish a new central website to provide information on CoC requirements. In particular, the United States has requested that the website : (a) list entities that Saudi Arabia has approved to test and certify products for the Saudi market; (b) set out the criteria and procedures that the Ministry of Commerce uses to recognize bodies to test and certify products for the Saudi market; (c) set out clear procedures for approved bodies to follow when issuing conformity certificates or marks to convey that a product complies with the relevant Saudi requirements; (d) clarify when testing is required (*e.g.*, for each individual shipment or once for each product type); and (e) indicate whether those procedures will change if Saudi Arabia adopts the conformity assessment scheme being developed by the Gulf Standards Organization.

The United States has also requested information from SASO, which is an affiliate member of the ILAC MRA, on how it is promoting acceptance of the ILAC MRA in Saudi Arabia. The United States has asked, in particular, for information on whether SASO takes into account whether a conformity assessment body has been accredited by an ILAC MRA signatory in determining whether to enter into an MRA with that body.

South Africa

Bilateral Engagement

The United States discusses TBT matters with South Africa during TBT Committee meetings and bilaterally on the margins of these meetings, as well as in the U.S.-South Africa Agreement Concerning the Development of Trade and Investment.

Liqueurs – Alcohol Content Restrictions

U.S. industry has expressed concerns about South Africa's standards for alcohol levels in certain alcoholic beverages, asserting that South Africa sets and applies those standards in a manner that excludes and discriminates against foreign alcoholic beverages. South Africa classifies "liqueurs" as beverages having a minimum alcohol content of 24 percent and classifies "spirit coolers" as beverages having 15 percent or less alcohol by volume. On the other hand, South Africa does not maintain any classification for spirit-based alcoholic beverages with an alcohol content of between 15-24 percent, with the exception of products that fall into the "Cream Liqueur" classification, namely spirit based alcoholic beverages that contain a dairy product. As a result, any U.S. products that fall into this range cannot be sold in South Africa.

Not only have these requirements kept certain U.S. products out of the market, but industry has reported that South Africa may not be applying its requirements equally to domestic and imported products. In particular, U.S. industry has reported that South Africa has granted at least one exception to its requirements for domestic products.

During 2011, the United States will continue to investigate U.S. industry concerns with South Africa's alcoholic beverage standards and, if appropriate, will urge South Africa to eliminate or modify its "liqueur" definition so that U.S. alcoholic beverage producers can sell their products in South Africa.

Taiwan

Bilateral Engagement

The United States discusses TBT matters with Taiwan during TBT Committee meetings and bilaterally on the margins of these meetings.

Ceiling Panels – Requirements for Incombustibility Testing Methods

U.S. companies that manufacture finished interior building materials, such as ceiling panels and wood paneling, have raised concerns regarding the test method that Taiwan mandates for determining whether those materials meet applicable incombustibility requirements. Industry has complained that Taiwan's current test method for ceiling panel incombustibility, which is similar to the current ISO standard, results in inconsistent and inaccurate incombustibility measures because the ISO standard was not meant to be applied to the testing of ceiling tiles. As a result, ceiling tiles manufactured in the United States are given a lower incombustibility rating than is otherwise warranted and, in some instances, fail the test altogether.

The United States has raised these concerns with Taiwan, including on the margins of the TBT Committee meeting in November 2009. In response, Taiwan's Bureau of Standards, Metrology, and Inspection (BSMI) has indicated it would consider adopting a new ISO standard when it is approved. In the meantime, Taiwan has indicated that it is open to accepting, an alternative approach, including using an Underwriters Laboratories (UL) certification of ceiling tile manufacturing plants if U.S. firms provide additional information on the UL certification process and permit BSMI to visit their U.S. plants.

Commodity Goods – Labeling Requirements

U.S. industry continues to express concern that Taiwan requires all "commodity goods" to be labeled with the manufacturer's or producer's name, telephone number, and address. In addition to concerns over protecting proprietary information, industry notes that some commodity goods may be produced by several different manufacturers, and product labels may not be large enough to contain each name, address, and phone number. The U.S. officials have raised these concerns with Taiwanese representatives, including on the margins of the TBT Committee meeting in November 2009. Taiwan is working to revise the relevant labeling requirements for textiles, garments, and 3C (computer, communication, and consumer electronics) information products. The United States will continue monitor Taiwan's progress is addressing this issue.

Product Multipacks – Labeling Requirements

In March 2009 U.S. industry raised concerns over a reinterpretation by Taiwan's Ministry of Economic Affairs (MOEA) of its Commodity Inspection Act and Commodity Labeling Act to require all units included in a retail multipack to be labeled, even if the retailer will not divide up the multipack for sale as single units. For example, the new rules will require a country of origin label for each pair of socks included within a sock multipack, even when the socks are sold as a six-pack. U.S. suppliers have asserted that this requirement imposes unnecessary additional costs as it will force them to add additional labels on their products to continue exporting to Taiwan.

U.S. officials raised this issue with their Taiwanese counterparts during the November 2009 TBT Committee, as well as on the margins of that meeting, and then followed up with questions during the WTO's review in 2010 of Taiwan's trade policies. Taiwan officials have responded that Taiwanese consumers typically purchase bulk items such as socks in individual units rather than multipacks so individual units included in multipacks must be labeled to avoid the risk of fraudulent country of origin labeling. U.S. officials have requested Taiwan to notify the WTO of its revised labeling rules, which will an opportunity for WTO Members to comment. MOEA is currently considering the request.

Thailand

Bilateral Engagement

The United States discusses TBT matters with Thailand during, and on the margins of, meetings of the TBT Committee as well as in bilateral dialogues such as the Thailand TIFA Council and the Bilateral Consultative Mechanism. Thailand also participates actively in APEC on standards and conformity assessment issues.

Alcoholic Beverages – Labeling Requirements

In January 2010, Thailand notified the WTO of a proposed regulation that would require alcohol beverage labels to include warning statements and photo images. The images would graphically depict certain potential adverse consequences of consuming alcohol, such as road accidents and diseased organs. The draft regulation also specifies that at least 50 percent of one side of square shaped packaging, or 30 percent of round or cylindrical shaped packages, must be allocated for the warning statements and images. In addition, the draft regulation calls for the various sets of warning labels and images to be rotated every 1,000 packages.

The United States raised concerns about the draft regulation during both the June and November 2010 TBT Committee meetings. Australia, Brazil, Chile, the EU, Mexico, New Zealand, and Switzerland expressed concerns as well. During the June TBT Committee meeting, Thailand distributed a report entitled "Why Thailand Should Have the Pictorial Warning Label on

Alcoholic Beverage Packages: A Technical Report, June 2010." Thailand said that it would accept comments on the report through its TBT Inquiry Point.

In its comments on Thailand's proposed labeling requirements, the United States requested Thailand to lay out the scientific basis for the specific warning statements it sought to require on alcoholic beverage packages. The United States also expressed concerns that the proposed size of the warning label in proportion to the size of the container would interfere with displaying legitimate trademarks and useful consumer information on alcoholic beverage containers, such as information necessary to distinguish one product from another. The United States also indicated that the requirement to rotate warning statements every 1,000 bottles could impose an onerous and potentially trade restrictive burden on producers, and was potentially unnecessary to achieve Thailand's objective of addressing the harms associated with alcohol consumption. In light of the scale of the proposed changes, the United States asked Thailand to lengthen the implementation period for regulation. Thailand responded that it was considering the U.S. concerns and that it would provide a reply as soon as one was available.

In September 2010, the U.S. Department of Agriculture hosted Thai officials in Washington to share best practices for encouraging responsible drinking, including best practices for warning labels. The United States will continue to engage Thailand on this issue in 2011.

"Snack Food" – Labeling Requirement

Thailand has imposed problematic labeling requirements for snack foods. Thailand requires snack foods to be labeled with a message stating: "Should consume small amounts, and exercise for a better health." While this labeling requirement represents a significant improvement over a labeling requirement that Thailand proposed in 2006, which would have instituted "traffic light" labeling meant to indicate the risks associated with certain categories of products, the United States remains concerned that the new requirement deviates from the prevailing scientific and technical information on health and nutrition. Further, Thailand's requirement creates a strong potential of impeding U.S. exports of these products.

The United States has engaged with Thailand on its snack food labeling rules since it announced its first proposal in 2006. The United States will continue to raise these requirements and other Thai food labeling regulations with Thai authorities with a view to ensuring that Thai requirements are based on relevant scientific and technical information on diet and nutrition and adopt an approach that encourages better health while avoiding trade disruption. To this end, the United States hosted a team of Thai regulatory officials in November 2010, to provide information about the U.S. food labeling system.

Turkey

Bilateral Engagement

The United States discusses standards-related issues with Turkey during TBT Committee meetings and bilaterally on the margins of those meetings. The United States also discusses these issues under the U.S. - Turkey Trade and Investment Framework Agreement (TIFA) and in the newly established bilateral ministerial level Framework for Strategic Economic and Commercial Cooperation (FSECC). The FSECC is co-chaired on the U.S. side by Ambassador Kirk and

Secretary of Commerce Gary Locke and on the Turkish side by Deputy Prime Minister Ali Babacan and Minister of Trade Zafer Caglayan. The FSECC is designed to reinforce the work of several bilateral sub-cabinet level dialogues on economic matters (including under the USTR-led TIFA) and to provide political-level guidance on particularly challenging commercial and economic issues.

Conformity Assessment Requirements

In recent years, Turkey has published a series of communiqués in its Official Gazette requiring certificates of conformity for certain types of products imported from outside the EU and requiring those products to undergo product safety inspections before they clear customs. Since these requirements were first published in December 2008, Turkey has revised them annually. The communiqués now in force include No. 2011/8 – radios and telecommunications equipment; 2011/9, which covers a broad range of "high risk products," such as machinery, to be inspected by the Turkish Standards Institute; 2011/10 – toys; 2011/11 – personal protective equipment; 2011/14 – building materials; 2011/15 – batteries; and 2011/16 – medical equipment. Turkey has not notified any of these measures to the WTO.

The United States is concerned about numerous aspects of these measures, including the fact that they do not apply to domestically-manufactured products or products originating in the EU. In addition, Turkey has not explained its rationale for adopting the import measures, has not revealed its product inspection criteria, and has not explained it compiled the list of products to which the measures apply. U.S. industry has reported that the measures are affecting numerous U.S. exports and that the time required for customs clearance has increased significantly. U.S. suppliers also contend that the paperwork requirements associated with the requirements are both redundant and costly.

The United States has raised concerns with Turkey both bilaterally and in the TBT Committee regarding its import inspection and certification requirements and pressed Turkey to reduce customs clearance times. U.S. officials have also urged Turkey to notify the relevant measures to the WTO and to provide stakeholders with an opportunity to provide comments and a reasonable period for implementation. The United States will continue to engage with Turkey on in 2011.

Food and Feed Products – Mandatory Biotech Labeling

In 2009, Turkey's Ministry of Agriculture published a regulation governing biotechnology in food and feed that did not have to be approved by the Parliament. The measure was neither made public nor notified to the WTO in advance, and contained no phase-in period. Turkey published an amended regulation in early 2010. The amended regulation is nearly identical to the original regulation and likewise contained no phase-in period (*i.e.,* it became effective on the date of publication. In August 2010, Turkey notified the regulation to the WTO.

Turkey's regulation mandates the labeling of bio-engineered ingredients in all food and feed in if the biotech content exceeds a certain threshold, a requirement that may could impede U.S. food and feed exports to Turkey. In addition, Turkey's regulation goes beyond mandatory method-of-production labeling by requiring that "GMO" labels on food should contain health warnings if the biotechnology food differs from the non-biotechnology food.

This labeling requirement raises additional concerns because it appears to presume that food containing biotechnology products that is different from its non-biotechnology food counterpart raises a health risk beyond that of its non-biotechnology counterpart. In fact, however, a biotechnology food might be different from a non-biotechnology food in ways that do not convey health risks; consequently, such health warnings would unnecessarily cause public alarm while providing no additional public health protection. For example, changes in oil composition could lead to health benefits, and the oil could still be as safe for consumption as similar oils. Thus, the use of health warnings in the absence of a legitimate health concern could misinform the public about the safety of the food.

The United States has repeatedly raised concerns about Turkey's labeling requirement during meetings of the TBT Committee and bilaterally and will continue to do so in 2011.

Medical Devices – Reimbursement and Regulatory Requirements

The United States has concerns with Turkey's new medical device reimbursement regulation, Communiqué SUT 2010/16, which appears to add a duplicative regulatory burden. Turkey's Ministry of Health has long had sole responsibility for the regulation of medical devices. However, beginning June 15, 2010 Turkey is requiring producers of medical devices used in spinal, orthopedic arthroplasty, and traumatology procedures to comply with regulations administered by Turkey's Social Security Institute as well. Turkey's new regulation requires medical device producers to supply additional documentation to maintain current reimbursement levels. If a medical device producer does not comply with these new regulations by the end of 2010, Turkey would cancel all reimbursements.

Turkey's has asserted that it requires this additional documentation for quality assurance purposes. It is unclear how the additional documentation will help achieve this objective, however, in light of the fact that Turkey's Ministry of Health, which oversees medical device safety and efficacy, does not require such documentation.

The United States has urged Turkey to notify its new requirements to the WTO, to meet with industry stakeholders so that they can share their concerns, and to take action to eliminate or modify any documentation requirements that are not needed to satisfy the requirements of Turkey's Medical Device Directive. Turkey has not yet responded to these requests, and the United States will continue to engage with Turkey on this issue in 2011.

Olive Oil and Olive Pomace Oil – Quality and Identity Standards

On September 2, 2010, Turkey's Ministry of Agriculture and Rural Affairs notified a proposed "Turkish Food Codex Communiqué on Olive Oil and Olive Pomace Oil" to the WTO. The proposal defines the characteristics necessary for a vegetable oil to be labeled as "olive oil" or "olive pomace oil." The proposal sets limits for the presence of fatty acids (*e.g.* linolenic acid) and campesterol that are characteristic of olive oil produced in the Mediterranean region, but do not take into account variations in olive oil arising from climate and soil conditions outside the Mediterranean. As a result, this proposal would not allow products derived from olives grown outside the Mediterranean region to be classified as "olive oil" or "olive pomace oil," which could adversely impact U.S. exports of olive oil.

The United States will engage Turkey on this issue in 2011.

Pharmaceuticals – GMP Decree

In late 2009, Turkey's Ministry of Health issued a "Regulation to Amend the Regulation on the Pricing of Medicinal Products for Human Use," which took effect on March 1, 2010. The regulation requires foreign pharmaceutical producers, as a condition of exporting their products to Turkey, to secure a Good Manufacturing Practice (GMP) certificate based on a plant inspection by Turkish authorities. The requirement does not apply if the country of manufacture is a party to an MRA with Turkey.

While it does not oppose inspection requirements for pharmaceutical manufacturing facilities, the United States has raised several concerns about this measure with Turkey. First, the United States expressed concerns that Turkey did not publish or notify the regulation to the WTO. Second, the United States expressed concerns that Turkey did not initially identify any health or safety issue arising from imports from the United States or other countries that prompted it to discontinue accepting GMP certificates issued by foreign regulatory authorities, such as the U.S. Food and Drug Administration. After several requests, Turkey provided the United States with a list of recalled U.S. pharmaceutical products, which it claims was the impetus for its regulations. The United States noted that while some U.S. pharmaceutical products have been the subject of recalls, the recalls should be viewed as a sign that the current U.S assurance system   is   working.

U.S. industry also raised concerns about Turkey's inspection requirement, including the fact that numerous approvals are pending and Turkey may not have sufficient capacity to inspect all of the manufacturing plants that need to be inspected in the near future. Given the apparent lack of inspection capacity, the United States is concerned that the process for obtaining approval could take several years, effectively precluding U.S. exports of important pharmaceutical products to Turkey.

In 2010, the United States used various opportunities to raise its concerns over the new inspection requirement with Turkey, and will continue to do so in 2011. The United States has urged Turkey to take immediate steps to restore access for safe, high quality U.S. pharmaceuticals to the Turkish market, including by promptly processing registration applications that U.S. producers submitted before March 2010 and giving priority to innovative drug applications that offer new medicinal therapies for Turkish patients.

Vietnam

Bilateral Engagement

The United States discusses standards-related issue with Vietnam during TBT Committee meetings and on the margins of TPP negotiations, as well as through the bilateral U.S. – Vietnam Trade and Investment Framework Agreement (TIFA) Council, which meets regularly and serves as a forum for raising and resolving trade and investment issues and for promoting increased technical cooperation activities. The United States has also partnered with Vietnam in advancing standards and conformity assessment issues in APEC.

Alcoholic Beverages – Food Safety Regulations for Alcohol

On March 24, 2010, Vietnam notified the WTO about a proposed regulation on food safety for alcoholic beverages. The proposed regulation specified the management and technical requirements relating to raw materials for processing alcoholic beverages, including chemical and microbiological parameters, heavy metals, and food additive and labeling requirements. Vietnam's proposal also required a compliance certification stamp and imposed new inspection and testing requirements for products covered by the regulation.

On May 19, 2010, the United States submitted comments to Vietnam, expressing concerns with numerous aspects of the proposal, including the proposed maximum level for aldehydes in distilled spirits of 5 mg per liter of pure alcohol. Standards of identity for spirits in most international markets are based on raw materials and production processes, not the chemical composition of the product. As such, these standards typically do not contain limits on aldehydes. In its comments, the United States also raised concerns about other aspects of Vietnam's proposal and asked Vietnam for clarification on the compliance certification stamp requirement as well as the new inspection and testing requirements.

In response to U.S. concerns, Vietnam withdrew its proposed maximum level for aldehydes in most distilled spirits in December 2010. However, Vietnam did not immediately withdraw this requirement for vodka, which affected up to $3.5 million in U.S. exports to Vietnam in 2010. U.S. officials continued to press Vietnam on this issue at the TBT Committee. Finally, in March 2011, Vietnam published revised regulations removing the maximum aldehyde level for vodka as well.

Despite this positive development, the United States remains concerned about certain aspects of Vietnam's new requirements, including the product certification requirement, the frequency of testing, the process to obtain certificates, differences in certificate grades, and uncertainty regarding the applicability of the compliance certification stamp to various products. The United States will continue to press Vietnam to address remaining concerns with Vietnam's regulations in 2011.

Biotechnology – Mandatory Labeling

In June 2010, Vietnam adopted a new food safety law, which requires labeling for biotech food products and that may impede exports of U.S. food products to Vietnam. Vietnam clarified these requirements with several implementing regulations it adopted in 2010. As specified under these regulations, the labeling requirement will only apply to certain types of GM foods, although Vietnamese officials have yet to identify those categories. The United States is concerned that Vietnam's labeling requirement, like other mandatory biotech labeling requirements, could increase consumer prices and product choices. Because Vietnam has not set a percentage or other threshold that will trigger its labeling requirement, it remains difficult to gauge the impact of the law on U.S. exports to Vietnam. The United States will continue to work closely with Vietnam on its biotech labeling law during 2011.

XII.   Appendix A: List of Commenters

Public comments received from:

1.   Advanced Medical Technology Association
2.   American Apparel and Footwear Association
3.   Distilled Spirits Council of the United States
4.   Grocery Manufacturers Association
5.   Harley Davidson Motor Company
6.   Herbalife International of America, Inc.
7.   International Intellectual Property Alliance
8.   National Association of Manufacturers
9.   National Electrical Manufacturers Association
10.   Pharmaceutical Research and Manufacturers of America
11.   Telecommunications Industry Association
12.   Toy Industry Association, Inc.
13.   Underwriters Laboratories
14.   Wine Institute
15.   Yum! Restaurants International

XIII.   Appendix B: List of Frequently Used Abbreviations and Acronyms

ANSI .... American National Standards Institute
APA.. Administrative Procedure Act of 1946
APEC .... Asia Pacific Economic Cooperation
EU .... European Union
FSCF .... Food Safety Cooperation Forum
FSCF PTIN .... Food Safety Cooperation Forum's Partnership Training Institute Network
FTA .... Free Trade Agreement
GATT.. General Agreement on Tariffs and Trade
IAF .... International Accreditation Forum
IEC... International Electrotechnical Commission
ILAC .... International Laboratory Accreditation Cooperation
ISO .... International Organization for Standardization
MRA .... Mutual Recognition Agreement
NAFTA .... North American Free Trade Agreement
NAMA .... Non-Agricultural Market Access
NEI... National Export Initiative
NIST.. National Institute of Standards and Technology
NTTAA .... National Technology Transfer and Advancement Act
NTB... Non-Tariff Barrier
NTE... National Trade Estimate Report on Foreign Trade Barriers
OECD.. Organization for Economic Cooperation and Development
OMB .... Office of Management and Budget
SCSC .... Subcommittee on Standards and Conformance
SDO.. Standards Developing Organization
SME .... Small and Medium Size Enterprise
SPS... Sanitary and Phytosanitary Measures
TAA .... Trade Agreements Act of 1979
TBT... Technical Barriers to Trade
TEC... United States – European Union Transatlantic Economic Council
TFTF .... Trade Facilitation Task Force
TIFA.. Trade and Investment Framework Agreement
TPP... Trans-Pacific Partnership
TPSC .... Trade Policy Staff Committee

USDA .... U.S. Department of Agriculture
USITC .... U.S. International Trade Commission
USTR .... Office of the United States Trade
Representative
WTO .... World Trade Organization